Oscar Wilde: Art and Morality

A Defence of "The Picture of Dorian Gray"

What the public calls an unhealthy novel is always a beautiful and healthy work of art.

Oscar Fingal O'Flahertie Wills Wilde was born on the 16th October 1854 in Dublin Ireland. The son of Dublin intellectuals Oscar proved himself an outstanding classicist at Dublin, then at Oxford. With his education complete Wilde moved to London and its fashionable cultural and social circles. With his biting wit, flamboyant dress, and glittering conversation, Wilde became one of the most well-known personalities of his day.

His only novel, The Picture of Dorian Gray was published in 1890 and he then moved on to writing for the stage with Salome in 1891. His society comedies produced enormous hits and turned him into one of the most successful writers of late Victorian London.

Whilst his masterpiece, The Importance of Being Earnest, was on stage in London, Wilde had the Marquess of Queensberry, the father of his lover, Lord Alfred Douglas, prosecuted for libel. The trial unearthed evidence that caused Wilde to drop his charges and led to his own arrest and trial for gross indecency. He was convicted and imprisoned for two years' hard labour. It was to break him.

On release he left for France, There he wrote his last work, The Ballad of Reading Gaol in 1898. He died destitute in Paris at the age of forty-six sipping champagne a friend had brought with the line 'Alas I am dying beyond my means'.

Here we publish his fascinating responses to the literary attacks on his masterpiece The Picture Of Dorian Gray.

Index Of Contents

MR ROBERT BUCHANAN ON PAGAN VICIOUSNESS
Oscar Wilde - A Short Biography

On the whole, an artist in England gains something by being attacked. His individuality is intensified. He becomes more completely himself. Of course, the attacks are very gross, very impertinent, and very contemptible. But then no artist expects grace from the vulgar mind, or style from the suburban intellect.

ART AND MORALITY - INTRODUCTION

"Why do you always write poetry? Why do you not write prose? Prose is so much more difficult."

These were the words of Walter Pater to Oscar Wilde on the occasion of their first meeting during the latter's undergraduate days at Oxford.[1] Those were "days of lyrical ardours and of studious sonnet-writing," wrote Wilde, in reviewing one of Pater's books some years later,[2] "days when one loved the exquisite intricacy and musical repetitions of the ballade, and the vilanelle with its linked long-drawn echoes and its curious completeness; days when one solemnly sought to discover the proper temper in which a triolet should be written; delightful days, in which, I am glad to say, there was far more rhyme than reason."

Oscar Wilde was never a voluminous writer, "writing bores me so," he once said to André Gide and at the time of which he speaks he had published little except some occasional verses in his University magazines. Then, in 1881, came his volume of collected poems, followed at intervals during the next nine or ten years by a collection of fairy stories and some essays in the leading reviews.

"I did not quite understand what Mr. Pater meant," he continues, "and it was not till I had carefully studied his beautiful and suggestive essays on the Renaissance that I fully realised what a wonderful self-conscious art the art of English prose-writing really is, or may be made to be."

It has been suggested that it was his late apprenticeship to an art that requires life-long study which rendered Wilde's prose so insincere, resembling more the conscious artifice of the modern French school than the restrained, yet jewelled style of Pater, whom he claimed as his master in prose.

It was not till 1890 that he published his first and only novel, The Picture of Dorian Gray, with its strangeness of colour and its passionate suggestion flickering like lightning through the gloom of the subject. The Puritans and the Philistines, who scented veiled improprieties in its paradoxes, were shocked; but it delighted the connoisseur and the artist, wearied as they were with the hum-drum accounts of afternoon tea parties and the love affairs of the curate.

That such a master of prose and scholarship as Pater should have written in terms of commendation of Dorian Gray is sufficient to prove how free from offence the story really is. In the original version of the story one passage struck Pater as being indefinite and likely to suggest evil to evil minds. This paragraph Wilde elaborated, but he refused to suppress a single sentence of what he had written. "No artist is consciously wrong," he declared.

A similar incident is recorded as early as 1878. Shairp, the Professor of Poetry at Oxford, suggested some improvements in Wilde's Newdigate Prize Poem Ravenna. Wilde listened to all the suggestions with courtesy, and even took notes of them, but he went away and had the poem printed without making a single alteration in it.

The Picture of Dorian Gray first appeared on June 20th, 1890, in Lippincott's Monthly Magazine for July. It was published in America by the J.B. Lippincott Company of Philadelphia simultaneously with the English edition of the same magazine issued by Messrs. Ward, Lock and Co.

A few weeks before the publication of his romance Wilde wrote a letter to a publisher stating that his story would appear in Lippincott's on the following 20th of June, and that after three months the copyright reverted to him. The publication of Dorian Gray would "create a sensation," he wrote; he was "going to add two additional chapters," and would the publishing house with whom he was corresponding care to consider it?

Unfortunately the letter bears no indication of the house to which it was sent. However, on the 1st of July in the following year The Picture of Dorian Gray was published in book form by Messrs. Ward, Lock and Co. In this form it contained seven new chapters. The binding was of a rough grey paper, the colour of cigarette ash, with back of parchment vellum. The gilt lettering and design was by Charles Ricketts. A sumptuous édition de luxe, limited to two hundred and fifty copies, signed by the author, was also issued, the covers being similar to the ordinary edition but the gilt tooling more elaborate.

In March, 1891, Wilde had written "A Preface to 'Dorian Gray'" in the Fortnightly Review, in which he enunciated his creed as an artist. This preface is included in all impressions of Dorian Gray which contain twenty chapters.

Wilde was indeed a true prophet when he foretold that his story would create a sensation. Though it occupied but a hundred pages in a monthly periodical, it was reviewed as fully as any chef d'oeuvre of a leading novelist. In one of his letters Wilde says that out of over two hundred press cuttings which he received in reference to Dorian Gray he took public notice of only three. But it is impossible to doubt but that he was thinking of his critics when he gave vent to his views on journalists, and the attitude of the British public towards art, in his essay on The Soul of Man a few months later. "A work of art is the unique result of a unique temperament," he writes. "Its beauty comes from the fact that the author is what he is.... The moment that an artist takes notice of what other people want, and tries to supply the demand, he ceases to be an artist."

He considers it to be an impertinence for the public (represented by the journalist) who knows nothing about art to criticise the artist and his work. In this country, he declares that the arts that have escaped best from the "aggressive, offensive and brutalising" attempts on the part of the public to interfere with the individual as an artist, are the arts in which the public takes no interest. He gives poetry as an instance, and declares that we have been able to have fine poetry because the public does not read it, and consequently does not influence it. But,

"In the case of the novel and the drama, arts in which the public does take an interest, the result of the exercise of popular authority has been absolutely ridiculous. No country produces such badly written fiction, such tedious, common work in the novel-form.... It must necessarily be so. The popular standard is of such a character that no artist can get to it. It is at once too easy and too difficult to be a popular novelist. It is too easy, because the requirements of the public as far as plot, style, psychology, treatment of life, and treatment of literature are concerned are within the reach of the very meanest capacity and the most uncultivated mind. It is too difficult, because to meet such requirements the artist would have to do violence to his temperament, would have to write not for the artistic joy of writing, but for the amusement of half-educated people, and so would have to suppress his individualism, forget his culture, annihilate his style, and surrender everything that is valuable in him....

"The one thing that the public dislikes is novelty. Any attempt to extend the subject-matter of art is extremely distasteful to the public; and yet the vitality and progress of art depend in a large measure on the continual extension of subject-matter. The public dislikes novelty because it is afraid of it.... A fresh mode of Beauty is absolutely distasteful to the public, and whenever it appears it gets so angry and bewildered that it always uses two stupid expressions, one is that the work of art is grossly unintelligible; the other, that the work of art is grossly immoral. When the public says a work is grossly unintelligible, it means that the artist has said a beautiful thing that is new; when the public describes a work as grossly immoral, it means that the artist has said or made a beautiful thing that is true. The former expression has reference to style; the latter to subject-matter. But it probably uses the words very vaguely, as an ordinary mob will use ready-made paving-stones. There is not a single real poet or prose-writer of this (the nineteenth) century on whom the British public has not solemnly conferred diplomas of immorality.... Of course, the public is very reckless in the use of the word.... An artist is, of course, not disturbed by it. The true artist is a man who believes absolutely in himself, because he is absolutely himself. But I can fancy that if an artist produced a work of art in England, that immediately on its appearance was recognised by the public, through its medium, which is the public press, as a work that was quite intelligible and highly moral, he would begin seriously to question whether in its creation he had really been himself at all, and consequently whether the work was not quite unworthy of him, and either of a thoroughly second-rate order or of no artistic value whatsoever."

Wilde then goes on to discuss the use of other words by journalists seeking to describe the work of an artist. These are the words "exotic," "unhealthy," and "morbid."[3] He disposes of each in turn. Briefly he says, that the public is morbid, the artist is never morbid. The word "exotic" merely expresses the rage of the momentary mushroom against the immortal, entrancing and exquisitely lovely orchid. "And," he concludes, "what the public calls an unhealthy novel is always a beautiful and healthy work of art."

[1] Oscar Wilde matriculated at Magdalen College, Oxford, October 17, 1874, and took his B.A. degree on November 28, 1878. Pater was at the time a Fellow and Tutor of Brasenose.

[2] The Speaker, Vol I., No. 12, page 319. March 22, 1890.

[3] The Times, February 23rd, 1893, in reviewing "Salome", said: "It is an arrangement in blood and ferocity, morbid, bizarre, repulsive and very offensive." Wilde replied (Times, March 2nd), "The opinions of English critics on a French work of mine have, of course, little, if any interest for me."

In The Soul of Man he wrote: "To call an artist morbid because he deals with morbidity as his subject matter, is as silly as if one called Shakespeare mad because he wrote 'King Lear.'"

       *   *   *   *   *

One of the results of the extraordinary tyranny of authority is that words
are absolutely distorted from their proper and simple meaning, and are used
to express the obverse of their right signification.

       *   *   *   *   *

A STUDY IN PUPPYDOM.[4]

Time was (it was in the '70's) when we talked about Mr. Oscar Wilde; time
came (it was in the '80's) when he tried to write poetry and, more
adventurous, we tried to read it; time is when we had forgotten him, or
only remember him as the late editor of the Woman's World, a part for which
he was singularly unfitted, if we are to judge him by the work which he has
been allowed to publish in Lippincott's Magazine, and which Messrs. Ward,
Lock and Co., have not been ashamed to circulate in Great Britain. Not
being curious in ordure, and not wishing to offend the nostrils of decent
persons, we do not propose to analyse "The Picture of Dorian Gray": that
would be to advertise the developments of an esoteric prurience. Whether
the Treasury or the Vigilance Society will think it worthwhile to prosecute
Mr. Oscar Wilde or Messrs. Ward, Lock and Co., we do not know; but on the
whole we hope they will not.

The puzzle is that a young man of decent parts, who enjoyed (when he was at
Oxford), the opportunity of associating with gentlemen, should put his name
(such as it is) to so stupid and vulgar a piece of work. Let nobody read it
in the hope of finding witty paradox or racy wickedness. The writer airs
his cheap research among the garbage of the French Décadents like any
drivelling pedant, and he bores you unmercifully with his prosy rigmaroles
about the beauty of the Body and the corruption of the Soul. The grammar is
better than Ouida's; the erudition equal: but in every other respect we
prefer the talented lady who broke off with "pious aposiopesis" when she
touched upon "the horrors which are described in the pages of Suetonius and
Livy", not to mention the yet worse infamies believed by many scholars to
be accurately portrayed in the lost works of Plutarch, Venus, and
Nicodemus, especially Nicodemus.

Let us take one peep at the young men in Mr. Oscar Wilde's story. Puppy No.
1 is the painter of the picture of Dorian Gray; Puppy No. 2 is the critic
(a courtesy lord, skilled in all the knowledge of the Egyptians and aweary
of all the sins and pleasures of London); Puppy No. 3 is the original,
cultivated by Puppy No. 1 with a "romantic friendship". The Puppies fall a-
talking: Puppy No. 1 about his art, Puppy No. 2 about his sins and
pleasures and the pleasures of sin, and Puppy No. 3 about himself, always
about himself, and generally about his face, which is "brainless and
beautiful". The Puppies appear to fill up the intervals of talk by plucking
daisies and playing with them, and sometimes by drinking "something with
strawberry in it." The youngest Puppy is told that he is charming; but he
mustn't sit in the sun for fear of spoiling his complexion. When he is
rebuked for being a naughty, wilful boy, he makes a pretty moue this man of
twenty! This is how he is addressed by the Blasé Puppy at their first
meeting:

"Yes, Mr. Gray, the gods have been good to you. But what the gods give they
quickly take away.... When your youth goes, your beauty will go with it,
and then you will suddenly discover that there are no triumphs left for
you.... Time is jealous of you, and wars against your lilies and roses. You
will become sallow, and hollow-cheeked, and dull-eyed. You will suffer
horribly."[5]

Why, bless our souls! haven't we read something of this kind somewhere in the classics? Yes, of course we have! But in what recondite author? Ah, yes, no, yes, it was in Horace! What an advantage it is to have received a classical education! And how it will astonish the Yankees! But we must not forget our Puppies, who have probably occupied their time in lapping "something with strawberry in it." Puppy No. 1 (the Art Puppy) has been telling Puppy No. 3 (the Doll Puppy) how much he admires him. What is the answer? "I am less to you than your ivory Hermes or your silver Faun. You will like them always. How long will you like me? Till I have my first wrinkle, I suppose. I know now that when one loses one's good looks, whatever they may be, one loses everything.... I am jealous of the portrait you have painted of me. Why should it keep what I must lose?... Oh, if it was only the other way! If the picture could only change, and I could be always what I am now!"[6]

No sooner said than done! The picture does change: the original doesn't. Here's a situation for you! Théophile Gautier could have made it romantic, entrancing, beautiful. Mr. Stevenson could have made it convincing, humorous, pathetic. Mr. Anstey could have made it screamingly funny. It has been reserved for Mr. Oscar Wilde to make it dull and nasty. The promising youth plunges into every kind of mean depravity, and ends in being "cut" by fast women and vicious men. He finishes with murder: the New Voluptuousness always leads up to blood-shedding, that is part of the cant. The gore and gashes wherein Mr. Rider Haggard takes a chaste delight are the natural diet for a cultivated palate which is tired of mere licentiousness. And every wickedness of filthiness committed by Dorian Gray is faithfully registered upon his face in the picture; but his living features are undisturbed and unmarred by his inward vileness. This is the story which Mr. Oscar Wilde has tried to tell; a very lame story it is, and very lamely it is told.

Why has he told it? There are two explanations; and, so far as we can see, not more than two. Not to give pleasure to his readers: the thing is too clumsy, too tedious, and alas! that we should say it, too stupid. Perhaps it was to shock his readers, in order that they might cry Fie! upon him and talk about him, much as Mr. Grant Allen recently tried in the Universal Review to arouse, by a licentious theory of the sexual relations, an attention which is refused to his popular chatter about other men's science. Are we then to suppose that Mr. Oscar Wilde has yielded to the craving for a notoriety which he once earned by talking fiddle faddle about other men's art, and sees his only chance of recalling it by making himself obvious at the cost of being obnoxious, and by attracting the notice which the olfactory sense cannot refuse to the presence of certain self-asserting organisms? That is an uncharitable hypothesis, and we would gladly abandon it. It may be suggested (but is it more charitable?) that he derives pleasure from treating a subject merely because it is disgusting. The phenomenon is not unknown in recent literature; and it takes two forms, in appearance widely separate, in fact, two branches from the same root, a root which draws its life from malodorous putrefaction. One development is found in the Puritan prurience which produced Tolstoi's "Kreutzer Sonata" and Mr. Stead's famous outbursts. That is odious enough and mischievous enough, and it is rightly execrated, because it is tainted with an hypocrisy not the less culpable because charitable persons may believe it to be unconscious. But is it more odious or more mischievous than the "frank Paganism" (that is the word, is it not?) which delights in dirtiness and confesses its delight? Still they are both chips from the same block, "The Maiden Tribute of Modern Babylon" and "The Picture of Dorian Gray", and both of them ought to be chucked into the fire. Not so much because they are dangerous and corrupt (they are corrupt but not dangerous) as because they are incurably silly, written by simple poseurs (whether they call themselves Puritan or Pagan) who know nothing about the life which they affect to have explored, and because they are mere catchpenny revelations of the non-existent, which, if they reveal anything at all, are revelations only of the singularly unpleasant minds from which they emerge.

[4] St. James's Gazette, June 24th, 1890.

[5] Pp. 16, 17.

[6] p. 19.

Who can help laughing when an ordinary journalist seriously proposes to limit the subject-matter at the disposal of the artist?

MR. WILDE'S BAD CASE.

To the Editor of the St. James's Gazette.[7]

Sir, I have read your criticism of my story, "The Picture of Dorian Gray," and I need hardly say that I do not propose to discuss its merits its demerits, its personalities or its lack of personality. England is a free country, and ordinary English criticism is perfectly free and easy.

Besides, I must admit that, either from temperament or taste, or from both, I am quite incapable of understanding how any work of art can be criticised from a moral standpoint. The sphere of art and the sphere of ethics are absolutely distinct and separate; and it is to the confusion between the two that we owe the appearance of Mrs. Grundy, that amusing old lady who represents the only original form of humour that the middle classes of this country have been able to produce.

What I do object to most strongly is that you should have placarded the town with posters on which was printed in large letters:

MR. OSCAR WILDE'S LATEST ADVERTISEMENT: A BAD CASE.

Whether the expression "A Bad Case" refers to my book or to the present position of the Government, I cannot tell. What was silly and unnecessary was the use of the term "advertisement".

I think I may say without vanity, though I do not wish to appear to run vanity down, that of all men in England I am the one who requires least advertisement. I am tired to death of being advertised, I feel no thrill when I see my name in a paper. The chronicle does not interest me anymore. I wrote this book entirely for my own pleasure, and it gave me very great pleasure to write it. Whether it becomes popular or not is a matter of absolute indifference to me. I am afraid, Sir, that the real advertisement is your cleverly written article. The English public, as a mass, takes no interest in a work of art until it is told that the work in question is immoral, and your réclame will, I have no doubt, largely increase the sale of the magazine; in which sale, I may mention, with some regret, I have no pecuniary interest.

I remain, Sir, your obedient servant,

OSCAR WILDE.

16, Tite Street, Chelsea, June 25th.

To this the following Editorial note was appended:

In the preceding column will be found the best reply which Mr. Oscar Wilde can make to our recent criticism of his mawkish and nauseous story, "The Picture of Dorian Gray". Mr. Wilde tells us that he is constitutionally unable to understand how any work of art can be criticised from a moral standpoint. We were quite aware that ethics and æsthetics are different matters, and that is why the greater part of our criticism was devoted not so much to the nastiness of "The Picture of Dorian Gray," but to its dulness and stupidity. Mr. Wilde pretends that we have advertised it. So we have, if any readers are attracted to a book which, we have warned them, will bore them insufferably.

That the story is corrupt cannot be denied; but we added, and assuredly believe, that it is not dangerous, because, as we said, it is tedious and stupid.

Mr. Wilde tells us that he wrote the story for his own pleasure, and found great pleasure in writing it. We congratulate him. There is no triumph more precious to your æsthete than the discovery of a delight which outsiders cannot share or even understand. The author of "The Picture of Dorian Gray" is the only person likely to find pleasure in it.

[7] June 26th, 1890.

Why should an artist be troubled by the shrill clamour of criticism?

MR. OSCAR WILDE AGAIN.

Mr. Oscar Wilde continues to carry on the defence of his novelette, "The Picture of Dorian Gray". Writing to us under yesterday's date[8], he says:

In your issue of to-day you state that my brief letter published in your columns is the "best reply" I can make to your article upon "Dorian Gray." This is not so. I do not propose to discuss fully the matter here, but I feel bound to say that your article contains the most unjustifiable attack that has been made upon any man of letters for many years.

The writer of it, who is quite incapable of concealing his personal malice, and so in some measure destroys the effect he wishes to produce, seems not to have the slightest idea of the temper in which a work of art should be approached. To say that such a book as mine should be "chucked into the fire" is silly. That is what one does with newspapers.

Of the value of pseudo-ethical criticism; in dealing with artistic work I have spoken already. But as your writer has ventured into the perilous grounds of literary criticism I ask you to allow me, in fairness not merely to myself, but to all men to whom literature is a fine art, to say a few words about his critical method.

He begins by assailing me with much ridiculous virulence because the chief personages in my story are puppies. They are puppies. Does he think that literature went to the dogs when Thackeray wrote about puppydom? I think that puppies are extremely interesting from an artistic as well as from a psychological point of view.

They seem to me to be certainly far more interesting than prigs; and I am of opinion that Lord Henry Wotton is an excellent corrective of the tedious ideal shadowed forth in the semi-theological novels of our age.

He then makes vague and fearful insinuations about my grammar and my erudition. Now, as regards grammar, I hold that, in prose at any rate, correctness should always be subordinate to artistic effect and musical cadence; and any peculiarities of syntax that may occur in "Dorian Gray" are deliberately intended, and are introduced to show the value of the artistic theory in question. Your writer gives no instance of any such peculiarity. This I regret, because I do not think that any such instances occur.

As regards erudition, it is always difficult, even for the most modest of us, to remember that other people do not know quite as much as one does one's self. I myself frankly admit I cannot imagine how a casual reference to Suetonius and Petronius Arbiter can be construed into evidence of a desire to impress an unoffending and ill-educated public by an assumption of superior knowledge. I should fancy that the most ordinary of scholars is perfectly well acquainted with the "Lives of the Cæsars" and with the "Satyricon."

"The Lives of the Cæsars," at any rate, forms part of the curriculum at Oxford for those who take the Honour School of "Literæ Humaniores"; and as for the "Satyricon" it is popular even among pass-men, though I suppose they are obliged to read it in translations.

The writer of the article then suggests that I, in common with that great and noble artist Count Tolstoi, take pleasure in a subject because it is dangerous. About such a suggestion there is this to be said. Romantic art deals with the exception and with the individual. Good people, belonging as they do to the normal, and so, commonplace type, are artistically uninteresting.

Bad people are, from the point of view of art, fascinating studies. They represent colour, variety and strangeness. Good people exasperate one's reason; bad people stir one's imagination. Your critic, if I must give him so honourable a title, states that the people in any story have no counterpart in life; that they are, to use his vigorous if somewhat vulgar phrase, "mere catchpenny revelations of the non-existent." Quite so.

If they existed they would not be worth writing about. The function of the artist is to invent, not to chronicle. There are no such people. If there were I would not write about them. Life by its realism is always spoiling the subject-matter of art.

The superior pleasure in literature is to realise the non-existent.

And, finally, let me say this. You have reproduced, in a journalistic form, the comedy of "Much Ado about Nothing" and have, of course, spoilt it in your reproduction.

The poor public, hearing from an authority so high as your own, that this is a wicked book that should be coerced and suppressed by a Tory Government, will, no doubt, rush to it and read it. But, alas, they will find that it is a story with a moral. And the moral is this: All excess, as well as all renunciation, brings its own punishment.

The painter, Basil Hallward, worshipping physical beauty far too much, as most painters do, dies by the hand of one in whose soul he has created a monstrous and absurd vanity. Dorian Gray, having led a life of mere sensation and pleasure, tries to kill conscience, and at that moment kills himself. Lord Henry Wotton seeks to be merely the spectator of life. He finds that those who reject the battle are more deeply wounded than those who take part in it.

Yes, there is a terrible moral in "Dorian Gray", a moral which the prurient will not be able to find in it, but it will be revealed to all whose minds are healthy. Is this an artistic error? I fear it is. It is the only error in the book.

The Editor added to this letter:

Mr. Oscar Wilde may perhaps be excused for being angry at the remarks which we allowed ourselves to make concerning the "moral tale" of the Three Puppies and the Magic Picture; but he should not misrepresent us. He says we suggested that his novel was a "wicked book which should be coerced and suppressed by a Tory Government." We did nothing of the kind. The authors of books of much less questionable character have been proceeded against by the Treasury or the Vigilance Society; but we expressly said that we hoped Mr. Wilde's masterpiece would be left alone.

Then, Mr. Wilde (like any young lady who has published her first novel "at the request of numerous friends") falls back on the theory of the critic's personal malice. This is unworthy of so experienced a literary gentleman. We can assure Mr. Wilde that the writer of that article had, and has, no "personal malice" or personal feeling towards him. We can surely censure a work which we believe to be silly and know to be offensive, without the imputation of malice, especially when that book is written by one who is so clearly capable of better things.

As for the critical question, Mr. Wilde is beating the air when he defends idealism and "romantic art" in literature. In the words of Mrs. Harris to Mrs. Gamp, "Who's deniging of it?"

Heaven forbid that we should refuse to an author the supreme pleasure of realising the non-existent; or that we should judge the "æsthetic" from the purely ethical standpoint.

No; our criticism starts from lower ground. Mr. Wilde says that his story is a moral tale, because the wicked persons in it come to a bad end. We will not be so rude as to quote a certain remark about morality which one Mr. Charles Surface made to Mr. Joseph Surface. We simply say that every critic has the right to point out that a work of art or literature is dull and incompetent in its treatment, as "The Picture of Dorian Gray" is, and that its dulness and incompetence are not redeemed because it constantly hints, not obscurely, at disgusting sins and abominable crimes, as "The Picture of Dorian Gray" does.

[8] June 26th.

A true artist takes no notice whatever of the public. The public is to him non-existent. He has no poppied or honeyed cakes through which to give the monster sleep or sustenance. He leaves that to the popular novelist.

MR. OSCAR WILDE'S DEFENCE.

To the Editor of the St. James's Gazette.[9]

Sir, As you still keep up, though in a somewhat milder form than before, your attacks on me and my book you not only confer upon me the right, but you impose on me the duty of reply.

You state, in your issue of to-day, that I misrepresented you when I said that you suggested that a book so wicked as mine should be "suppressed and coerced by a Tory Government." Now, you did not propose this, but you did suggest it. When you declare that you do not know whether or not the Government will take action about my book, and remark that the authors of books much less wicked have been proceeded against in law, the suggestion is quite obvious.

In your complaint of misrepresentation you seem to me, Sir, to have been not quite candid.

However, as far as I am concerned, this suggestion is of no importance. What is of importance is that the editor of a paper like yours should appear to countenance the monstrous theory that the Government of a country should exercise a censorship over imaginative literature. This is a theory against which I, and all men of letters of my acquaintance, protest most strongly; and any critic who admits the reasonableness of such a theory shows at once that he is quite incapable of understanding what literature is, and what are the rights that literature possesses. A Government might just as well try to teach painters how to paint, or sculptors how to model, as attempt to interfere with the style, treatment and subject-matter of the literary artist, and no writer, however eminent or obscure, should ever give his sanction to a theory that would degrade literature far more than any didactic or so-called immoral book could possibly do.

You then express your surprise that "so experienced a literary gentleman" as myself should imagine that your critic was animated by any feeling of personal malice towards him. The phrase "literary gentleman" is a vile phrase, but let that pass.

I accept quite readily your assurance that your critic was simply criticising a work of art in the best way that he could, but I feel that I was fully justified in forming the opinion of him that I did. He opened his article by a gross personal attack on myself. This, I need hardly say, was an absolutely unpardonable error of critical taste.

There is no excuse for it except personal malice; and you, Sir, should not have sanctioned it. A critic should be taught to criticise a work of art without making any reference to the personality of the author. This, in fact, is the beginning of criticism. However, it was not merely his personal attack on me that made me imagine that he was actuated by malice. What really confirmed me in my first impression was his reiterated assertion that my book was tedious and dull.

Now, if I were criticising my book, which I have some thoughts of doing, I think I would consider it my duty to point out that it is far too crowded with sensational incident, and far too paradoxical in style, as far, at any rate, as the dialogue goes. I feel that from a standpoint of art there are true defects in the book. But tedious and dull the book is not.

Your critic has cleared himself of the charge of personal malice, his denial and yours being quite sufficient in the matter; but he has done so only by a tacit admission that he has really no critical instinct about literature and literary work, which, in one who writes about literature is, I need hardly say, a much graver fault than malice of any kind.

Finally, Sir, allow me to say this. Such an article as you have published really makes me despair of the possibility of any general culture in England. Were I a French author, and my book brought out in Paris, there is not a single literary critic in France on any paper of high standing who would think for a moment of criticising it from an ethical standpoint. If he did so he would stultify himself, not merely in the eyes of all men of letters, but in the eyes of the majority of the public.

You have yourself often spoken against Puritanism. Believe me, Sir, Puritanism is never so offensive and destructive as when it deals with art matters. It is there that it is radically wrong. It is this Puritanism, to which your critic has given expression, that is always marring the artistic instinct of the English. So far from encouraging it, you should set yourself against it, and should try to teach your critics to recognise the essential difference between art and life.

The gentleman who criticised my book is in a perfectly hopeless confusion about it, and your attempt to help him out by proposing that the subject-matter of art should be limited does not mend matters. It is proper that limitation should be placed on action. It is not proper that limitation should be placed on art. To art belong all things that are and all things that are not, and even the editor of a London paper has no right to restrain the freedom of art in the selection of subject-matter.

I now trust, Sir, that these attacks on me and my book will cease. There are forms of advertisement that are unwarranted and unwarrantable.

I am, Sir, your obedient servant,

OSCAR WILDE.

16, Tite Street, S.W., June 27th.

[9] June 28th.

The public ... is always asking a writer why he does not write like somebody else ... quite oblivious of the fact that if he did anything of the kind he would cease to be an artist.

Once more the Editor attempted to justify his reviewer's trenchant criticism:

Mr. Oscar Wilde makes his third and, we presume, his final reply to the criticism which we published on "The Picture of Dorian Gray." Somewhat grudgingly, but in sufficiently explicit terms, he withdraws the charge of "personal malice" which he brought against the critic, and which, we may again assure him, is absolutely unfounded.

But he adheres to the other charge of critical incapacity. Mr. Wilde assures us that his book, so far from being dull and tedious, is full of interest; an opinion which is shared (see the letter we print on another page to-day) by his publishers' advertising agent-in-advance.

Well, we can only repeat that we disagree with Mr. Wilde and his publishers' paragraphist.

Quite apart from "ethical" considerations, the book seems to us a feeble and ineffective attempt at a kind of allegory which, in the hands of abler writers (writers like Mr. Stevenson and Mr. Anstey, for instance) can be made striking or amusing.

Mr. Wilde also says that we suggested that the author and publishers of "The Picture of Dorian Gray" ought to be prosecuted by the Tory Government, by which we presume he means the Treasury. No; we consider that such prosecutions are ill-advised, and expressly suggested that such action ought not to be taken against a book which we believed to be rendered innocuous by the tedious and stupid qualities which the critic discovered and explained. Secondly, Mr. Wilde hints that the "rights of literature" include a right to say what it pleases, how it pleases and where it pleases. That is a right not only not recognised by the law of the land, but expressly denied by penalties which have been repeatedly enforced. Then what does Mr. Oscar Wilde mean by talking about the "rights of literature"? We will not insult an artist, who is by his own account un-moral or supra-moral by suggesting that he means "moral rights." But he tells us that limitations may be set on action but ought not to be set on art. Quite so. But art becomes action when the work of art is published. It is offensive publications that we object to, not the offensive imaginings of such minds as find their pleasure therein.

LETTER FROM "A LONDON EDITOR."

In the same issue of June 28th appeared the following letter:

To the Editor of the St. James's Gazette.

Sir, If Mr. Oscar Wilde is the last man in England (according to his own account) who requires advertisement, his friends and publishers do not seem to be of the same opinion. Otherwise it is difficult to account for the following audacious puff-postive which has been sent through the halfpenny post to newspaper editors and others:

Mr. Oscar Wilde will contribute to the July number of Lippincott's Magazine a complete novel, entitled "The Picture of Dorian Gray," which, as the first venture in fiction of one of the most prominent personalities and artistic influences of the day, will be everywhere read with wide interest and curiosity. But the story is in itself so strong and strange, and so picturesque and powerful in style, that it must inevitably have created a sensation in the literary world, even if published without Mr. Wilde's name on the title page.

Viewed merely as a romance, it is from the opening paragraph down to the tragic and ghastly climax, full of strong and sustained interest; as a study in psychology it is phenomenal; judged even purely as a piece of literary workmanship it is one of the most brilliant and remarkable productions of the year.

Such, Sir, is the estimate of Mr. Wilde's publishers or paragraph writer. Note the adjectival exuberance of the puffer, complete, strong, strange, picturesque, powerful, tragic, ghastly, sustained, phenomenal, brilliant and remarkable. For a man who does not want advertisement this is not bad.

I am, Sir, your obedient servant,

June 27th.   A LONDON EDITOR.

The sphere of art and the sphere of ethics are absolutely distinct and separate.

MR. OSCAR WILDE'S DEFENCE.

To the Editor of the St. James's Gazette.[10]

Sir, In your issue of this evening you publish a letter from "A London Editor" which clearly insinuates in the last paragraph that I have in some way sanctioned the circulation of an expression of opinion, on the part of the proprietors of Lippincott's Magazine, of the literary and artistic value of my story of the "Picture of Dorian Gray."

Allow me, Sir, to state that there are no grounds for this insinuation. I was not aware that any such document was being circulated; and I have written to the agents, Messrs. Ward and Lock, who cannot, I feel sure, be primarily responsible for its appearance, to ask them to withdraw it at once. No publisher should ever express an opinion of the value of what he publishes. That is a matter entirely for the literary critic to decide.

I must admit, as one to whom contemporary literature is constantly submitted for criticism, that the only thing that ever prejudices me against a book is the lack of literary style; but I can quite understand how any ordinary critic would be strongly prejudiced against a work that was accompanied by a premature and unnecessary panegyric from the publisher. A publisher is simply a useful middle-man. It is not for him to anticipate the verdict of criticism.

I may, however, while expressing my thanks to the "London Editor" for drawing my attention to this, I trust, purely American method of procedure, venture to differ from him in one of his criticisms. He states that he regards the expression "complete" as applied to a story, as a specimen of the "adjectival exuberance of the puffer." Here, it seems to me, he sadly exaggerates. What my story is is an interesting problem. What my story is not is a "novelette", a term which you have more than once applied to it. There is no such word in the English language as novelette. It should not be used. It is merely part of the slang of Fleet Street.

In another part of your paper, Sir, you state that I received your assurance of the lack of malice in your critic "somewhat grudgingly." This is not so. I frankly said that I accepted that assurance "quite readily," and that your own denial and that of your critic were "sufficient."

Nothing more generous could have been said. What I did feel was that you saved your critic from the charge of malice by convicting him of the unpardonable crime of lack of literary instinct. I still feel that. To call my book an ineffective attempt at allegory that, in the hands of Mr. Anstey might have been made striking, is absurd.

Mr. Anstey's sphere in literature and my sphere are different.

You then gravely ask me what rights I imagine literature possesses. That is really an extraordinary question for the editor of a newspaper such as yours to ask. The rights of literature, Sir, are the rights of intellect.

I remember once hearing M. Renan say that he would sooner live under a military despotism than under the despotism of the Church, because the former merely limited the freedom of action, while the latter limited the freedom of mind.

You say that a work of art is a form of action: It is not. It is the highest mode of thought.

In conclusion, Sir, let me ask you not to force on me this continued correspondence by daily attacks. It is a trouble and a nuisance.

As you assailed me first, I have a right to the last word. Let that last word be the present letter, and leave my book, I beg you, to the immortality that it deserves.

I am, Sir, your obedient servant,

                    OSCAR WILDE.

16, Tite Street, S.W., June 28th.

"THE LAST WORD."

We should be sorry to deny the ex-editor of the Woman's World the feminine privilege of "the last word" for which he pleads to-day. At the same time we cannot admit that we force upon Mr. Oscar Wilde the burden of a newspaper controversy by "daily attacks."

Mr. Wilde published a book, and (presumably) submitted it to criticism: we exercised our rights as critics of contemporary literature by pointing out that we thought the book feeble and offensive. Mr. Wilde replies, defending his book against our unfavourable criticism, and we have again the right to point out that we do not consider that he has satisfactorily met our arguments and our objections. For the rest, we are quite willing to leave "The Picture of Dorian Gray" to the "immortality it deserves." We must add one word. We congratulate Mr. Wilde on his emphatic disavowal of the ridiculous puff preliminary which his publishers had chosen to circulate.

Two days later (July 2nd) the Editor could not resist one more word:

Modest Mr. Oscar Wilde. He has been having a little dispute with the Daily Chronicle as well as with the St. James's Gazette and this is what he writes to our contemporary:

My story is an essay on decorative art. It re-acts against the crude brutality of plain realism. It is poisonous, if you like, but you cannot deny that it is also perfect, and perfection is what we artists aim at.

[10] June 30th.

Art should never try to be popular. The public should try and make itself artistic.

"THE DAILY CHRONICLE"[11] ON "DORIAN GRAY."

Dullness and dirt are the chief features of Lippincott's this month. The element in it that is unclean, though undeniably amusing, is furnished by Mr. Oscar Wilde's story of "The Picture of Dorian Gray." It is a tale spawned from the leprous literature of the French Décadents, a poisonous book, the atmosphere of which is heavy with the mephitic odours of moral and spiritual putrefaction, a gloating study of the mental and physical corruption of a fresh, fair and golden youth, which might be horrible and fascinating but for its effeminate frivolity, its studied insincerity, its theatrical cynicism, its tawdry mysticism, its flippant philosophisings and the contaminating trail of garish vulgarity which is over all Mr. Wilde's elaborate Wardour-street æstheticism and obtrusively cheap scholarship.

Mr. Wilde says his book has "a moral." The "moral," so far as we can collect it, is that man's chief end is to develop his nature to the fullest by "always searching for new sensations," that when the soul gets sick the way to cure it is to deny the senses nothing, for "nothing," says one of Mr. Wilde's characters, Lord Henry Wotton, "can cure the soul but the senses, just as nothing can cure the senses but the soul." Man is half angel and half ape, and Mr. Wilde's book has no real use if it be not to inculcate the "moral" that when you feel yourself becoming too angelic you cannot do better than rush out and make a beast of yourself. There is not a single good and holy impulse of human nature, scarcely a fine feeling or instinct that civilization, art and religion have developed throughout the ages as part of the barriers between Humanity and Animalism that is not held up to ridicule and contempt in "Dorian Gray," if, indeed, such strong words can be fitly applied to the actual effect of Mr. Wilde's airy levity and fluent impudence. His desperate effort to vamp up a "moral" for the book at the end is, artistically speaking, coarse and crude, because the whole incident of Dorian Gray's death is, as they say on the stage, "out of the picture." Dorian's only regret is that unbridled indulgence in every form of secret and unspeakable vice, every resource of luxury and art, and sometimes still more piquant to the jaded young man of fashion, whose lives "Dorian Gray" pretends to sketch, by every abomination of vulgarity and squalor is what? Why, that it will leave traces of premature age and loathsomeness on his pretty facy, rosy with the loveliness that endeared youth of his odious type to the paralytic patricians of the Lower Empire.

Dorian Gray prays that a portrait of himself which an artist (who raves about him as young men do about the women they love not wisely but too well) has painted may grow old instead of the original. This is what happens by some supernatural agency, the introduction of which seems purely farcical, so that Dorian goes on enjoying unfading youth year after year, and might go on forever using his senses with impunity "to cure his soul," defiling English society with the moral pestilence which is incarnate in him, but for one thing. That is his sudden impulse not merely to murder the painter, which might be artistically defended on the plea that it is only a fresh development of his scheme for realizing every phase of life-experience, but to rip up the canvas in a rage, merely because, though he had permitted himself to do one good action, it had not made his portrait less hideous. But all this is inconsistent with Dorian Gray's cool, calculating, conscienceless character, evolved logically enough by Mr Wilde's "New Hedonism."

Then Mr. Wilde finishes his story by saying that on hearing a heavy fall Dorian Gray's servants rushed in, found the portrait on the wall as youthful looking as ever, its senile ugliness being transferred to the foul profligate himself, who is lying on the floor stabbed to the heart. This is a sham moral, as indeed everything in the book is a sham, except the one element in the book which will taint every young mind that comes in contact with it. That element is shockingly real, and it is the plausibly insinuated defence of the creed that appeals to the senses "to cure the soul" whenever the spiritual nature of man suffers from too much purity and self-denial.

The rest of this number of Lippincott consists of articles of harmless padding.

When critics disagree the artist is in accord with himself.

OSCAR WILDE'S REPLY.

"DORIAN GRAY."

To the Editor of the Daily Chronicle.[12]

Sir, Will you allow me to correct some errors into which your critic has
fallen in his review of my story, "The Picture of Dorian Gray," published
in to-day's issue of your paper?

Your critic states, to begin with, that I make desperate attempts to "vamp
up" a moral in my story. Now I must candidly confess that I do not know
what "vamping" is. I see, from time to time, mysterious advertisements in
the newspapers about "How to Vamp," but what vamping really means remains a
mystery to me, a mystery that, like all other mysteries, I hope someday to
explore.

However, I do not propose to discuss the absurd terms used by modern
journalism. What I want to say is that, so far from wishing to emphasise
any moral in my story, the real trouble I experienced in writing the story
was that of keeping the extremely obvious moral subordinate to the artistic
and dramatic effect.

When I first conceived the idea of a young man selling his soul in exchange
for eternal youth, an idea that is old in the history of literature, but to
which I have given new form, I felt that, from an æsthetic point of view,
it would be difficult to keep the moral in its proper secondary place; and
even now I do not feel quite sure that I have been able to do so. I think
the moral too apparent. When the book is published in a volume I hope to
correct this defect.

As for what the moral is, your critic states that it is this, that when a
man feels himself becoming "too angelic" he should rush out and make a
"beast of himself." I cannot say that I consider this a moral. The real
moral of the story is that all excess, as well as all renunciation, brings
its punishment, and this moral is so far artistically and deliberately
suppressed that it does not enunciate its law as a general principle, but
realises itself purely in the lives of individuals, and so becomes simply a
dramatic element in a work of art, and not the object of the work of art
itself.

Your critic also falls into error when he says that Dorian Gray, having a
"cool, calculating, conscienceless character," was inconsistent when he
destroyed the picture of his own soul, on the ground that the picture did
not become less hideous after he had done what, in his vanity, he had
considered his first good action. Dorian Gray has not got a cool,
calculating, conscienceless character at all. On the contrary, he is
extremely impulsive, absurdly romantic, and is haunted all through his life
by an exaggerated sense of conscience which mars his pleasures for him and
warns him that youth and enjoyment are not everything in the world. It is
finally to get rid of the conscience that had dogged his steps from year to
year that he destroys the picture; and thus in his attempt to kill
conscience Dorian Gray kills himself.

Your critic then talks about "obtrusively cheap scholarship." Now, whatever a scholar writes is sure to display scholarship in the distinction of style and the fine use of language; but my story contains no learned or pseudo-learned discussions, and the only literary books that it alludes to are books that any fairly educated reader may be supposed to be acquainted with, such as the "Satyricon" of Petronius Arbiter, or Gautier's "Emaux et Camées." Such books as Le Conso's "Clericalis Disciplina" belong not to culture, but to curiosity. Anybody may be excused for not knowing them.

Finally, let me say this, the æsthetic movement produced certain curious colours, subtle in their loveliness and fascinating in their almost mystical tone. They were, and are, our reaction against the crude primaries of a doubtless more respectable but certainly less cultivated age. My story is an essay on decorative art. It re-acts against the crude brutality of plain realism. It is poisonous, if you like, but you cannot deny that it is also perfect, and perfection is what we artists aim at.

I remain, Sir, your obedient servant,

OSCAR WILDE.

16, Tite Street, June 30th.

[12] July 2nd, 1890.

We allow absolute freedom to the journalist, and entirely limit the artist. English public opinion, that is to say, tries to constrain and impede and warp the man who makes things that are beautiful in effect, and compels the journalist to retail things that are ugly, or disgusting, or revolting in fact, so that we have the most serious journalists in the world, and the most indecent newspapers.

"THE SCOTS OBSERVER'S" REVIEW.

The following diatribe is from a journal, The Scots Observer[13], which had an ephemeral existence in the early 'nineties. Under the heading of "Reviews and Magazines" it launched forth in these words:

"Why go grubbing in muck heaps? The world is fair, and the proportion of healthy-minded men and honest women to those that are foul, fallen or unnatural is great. Mr. Oscar Wilde has again been writing stuff that were better unwritten; and while "The Picture of Dorian Gray," which he contributes to Lippincott's, is ingenious, interesting, full of cleverness, and plainly the work of a man of letters, it is false art for its interest is medico-legal; it is false to human nature, for its hero is a devil; it is false to morality, for it is not made sufficiently clear that the writer does not prefer a course of unnatural iniquity to a life of cleanliness, health and sanity. The story, which deals with matters only fitted for the Criminal Investigation Department or a hearing in camera, is discreditable alike to author and editor.

Mr. Wilde has brains, and art, and style; but, if he can write for none but outlawed noblemen and perverted telegraph-boys, the sooner he takes to tailoring (or some other decent trade) the better for his own reputation and the public morals."

[13] July 5th, 1890.

The Scots Observer was edited by W.E. Henley. It was violently Tory in character, and afterwards became The National Observer, but not even a re-christening could save it from an early death.

We are dominated by journalism.... Journalism governs forever and ever.

OSCAR WILDE'S REPLIES.

To this vulgar abuse Wilde condescended to reply in the following terms:

16, Tite Street, Chelsea,

9th July, 1890.

Sir, You have published a review of my story, "The Picture of Dorian Gray." As this review is grossly unjust to me as an artist, I ask you to allow me to exercise in your columns my right of reply.

Your reviewer, Sir, while admitting that the story in question is "plainly the work of a man of letters," the work of one who has "brains, and art, and style," yet suggests, and apparently in all seriousness, that I have written it in order that it should be read by the most depraved members of the criminal and illiterate classes. Now, Sir, I do not suppose that the criminal and illiterate classes ever read anything except newspapers. They are certainly not likely to be able to understand anything of mine. So let them pass, and on the broad question of why a man of letters writes at all let me say this.

The pleasure that one has in creating a work of art is a purely personal pleasure, and it is for the sake of this pleasure that one creates. The artist works with his eye on the object. Nothing else interests him. What people are likely to say does not even occur to him.

He is fascinated by what he has in hand. He is indifferent to others. I write because it gives me the greatest possible artistic pleasure to write. If my work pleases the few, I am gratified. If it does not, it causes me no pain. As for the mob, I have no desire to be a popular novelist. It is far too easy.

Your critic then, Sir, commits the absolutely unpardonable crime of trying to confuse the artist with his subject-matter. For this, Sir, there is no excuse at all.

Of one who is the greatest figure in the world's literature since Greek days, Keats remarked that he had as much pleasure in conceiving the evil as he had in conceiving the good. Let your reviewer, Sir, consider the bearings of Keats' criticism, for it is under these conditions that every artist works. One stands remote from one's subject-matter. One creates it, and one contemplates it. The further away the subject-matter is, the more freely can the artist work.

Your reviewer suggests that I do not make it sufficiently clear whether I prefer virtue to wickedness or wickedness to virtue. An artist, Sir, has no ethical sympathies at all. Virtue and wickedness are to him simply what the colours on his palette are to the painter. They are no more, and they are no less. He sees that by their means a certain artistic effect can be produced and he produces it. Iago may be morally horrible and Imogen stainlessly pure. Shakespeare, as Keats said, had as much delight in creating the one as he had in creating the other.

It was necessary, Sir, for the dramatic development of this story, to surround Dorian Gray with an atmosphere of moral corruption. Otherwise the story would have had no meaning and the plot no issue. To keep this atmosphere vague and indeterminate and wonderful was the aim of the artist who wrote the story. I claim, Sir, that he has succeeded. Each man sees his own sin in Dorian Gray. What Dorian Gray's sins are no one knows. He who finds them has brought them.

In conclusion, Sir, let me say how really deeply I regret that you should have permitted such a notice, as the one I feel constrained to write on, to have appeared in your paper. That the editor of the St. James's Gazette should have employed Caliban as his art-critic was possibly natural. The editor of the Scots Observer should not have allowed Thersites to make mows in his reviews. It is unworthy of so distinguished a man of letters.

I am, etc.,

OSCAR WILDE.

To this letter the following editorial note was added:

It was not to be expected that Mr. Wilde would agree with his reviewer as to the artistic merit of his booklet. Let it be conceded to him that he has succeeded in surrounding his hero with such an atmosphere as he describes. This is his reward. It is none the less legitimate for a critic to hold and to express the opinion that no treatment, however skilful, can make the atmosphere tolerable to his readers. That is his punishment. No doubt, it is the artist's privilege to be nasty; but he must exercise that privilege at his peril.

During the next two weeks various correspondents aired their views on the subject, and in the third week[14] Oscar Wilde replied to them thus:

Sir, In a letter, dealing with the relations of art to morals, published in your columns, a letter which I may say seems to me in many respects admirable, especially in its insistence on the right of the artist to select his own subject-matter, Mr. Charles Whibley suggests that it must be peculiarly painful to me to find that the ethical import of "Dorian Gray" has been so strongly recognised by the foremost Christian papers of England and America that I have been greeted by more than one of them as a moral reformer.

Allow me, sir, to re-assure on this point not merely Mr. Charles Whibley himself, but also your, no doubt, anxious readers. I have no hesitation in saying that I regard such criticisms as a very gratifying tribute to my story. For if a work of art is rich and vital and complete, those who have artistic instincts will see its beauty, and those to whom ethics appeal more strongly than æsthetics will see its moral lesson. It will fill the cowardly with terror, and the unclean will see in it their own shame. It will be to each man what he is himself. It is the spectator, and not life, that art really mirrors.

And so in the case of "Dorian Gray," the purely literary critic, as in the Speaker and elsewhere, regards it as a "serious and fascinating work of art"[15]: the critic who deals with art in its relation to conduct, as the Christian Leader and the Christian World, regards it as an ethical parable: Light, which I am told is the organ of the English mystics, regards it as "a work of high spiritual import"[16]: the St. James's Gazette, which is seeking apparently to be the organ of the prurient, sees or pretends to see in it all kinds of dreadful things, and hints at Treasury prosecutions: and your Mr. Charles Whibley genially says that he discovers in it "lots of morality."

It is quite true that he goes on to say that he detects no art in it. But I do not think that it is fair to expect a critic to be able to see a work of art from every point of view. Even Gautier had his limitations just as much as Diderot had, and in modern England Goethes are rare. I can only assure Mr. Charles Whibley that no moral apotheosis to which he has added the most modest contribution could possibly be a source of unhappiness to an artist.

I remain, Sir, your obedient servant,

OSCAR WILDE

[14] *August 2nd.*
[15] *See ch. PROFUSE AND PERFERVID.*
[16] *See ch. "THE PICTURE OF DORIAN GRAY" - A Spiritualistic Review.*

When it (the public) says a work of art is grossly unintelligible, it means that the artist has said or made a beautiful thing that is new; when it describes a work as grossly immoral, it means that the artist has said or made a beautiful thing that is true. The former expression has reference to style; the latter to subject-matter.

This again led to further correspondence, and after an interval of two weeks Oscar Wilde returned to the charges levelled against his book and replied for the third and last time.[17] His letter dated from 16, Tite Street, Chelsea, 13th August, 1890, was as follows:

"Sir, I am afraid I cannot enter into any newspaper discussion on the subject of art with Mr. Whibley, partly because the writing of letters is always a trouble to me, and partly because I regret to say that I do not know what qualifications Mr. Whibley possesses for the discussion of so important a topic. I merely noticed his letter because (I am sure without in any way intending it) he made a suggestion about myself personally that was quite inaccurate. His suggestion was that it must have been painful to me to find that a certain section of the public, as represented by himself and the critics of some religious publications, had insisted on finding what he calls "lots of morality" in my story of "The Picture of Dorian Gray."

Being naturally desirous of setting your readers right on a question of such vital interest to the historian, I took the opportunity of pointing out in your columns that I regarded all such criticisms as a very gratifying tribute to the ethical beauty of the story, and I added that I was quite ready to recognise that it was not really fair to ask of any ordinary critic that he should be able to appreciate a work of art from every point of view.

I still hold this opinion. If a man sees the artistic beauty of a thing he will probably care very little for its ethical import. If his temperament is more susceptible to ethical than to æsthetic influences he will be blind to questions of style, treatment and the like. It takes a Goethe to see a work of art fully, completely and perfectly, and I thoroughly agree with Mr. Whibley when he says that it is a pity that Goethe never had an opportunity of reading "Dorian Gray." I feel quite certain that he would have been delighted by it, and I only hope that some ghostly publisher is even now distributing shadowy copies in the Elysian fields, and that the cover of Goethe's copy is powdered with gilt asphodels.

You may ask me, Sir, why I should care to have the ethical beauty of my story recognised. I answer simply because it exists, because the thing is there.

The chief merit of Madame Bovary is not the moral lesson that can be found in it, any more than the chief merit of Salammbô is its archæology; but Flaubert was perfectly right in exposing the ignorance of those who called the one immoral and the other inaccurate; and not merely was he right in the ordinary sense of the word, but he was artistically right, which is everything. The critic has to educate the public; the artist has to educate the critic.

Allow me to make one more correction, Sir, and I will have done with Mr. Whibley. He ends his letter with the statement that I have been indefatigable in my public appreciation of my own work. I have no doubt that in saying this he means to pay me a compliment, but he really over-rates my capacity, as well as my inclination for work. I must frankly confess that, by nature and by choice, I am extremely indolent.

Cultivated idleness seems to me to be the proper occupation for men. I dislike newspaper controversies of any kind, and of the two hundred and sixteen criticisms of "Dorian Gray," that have passed from my library table into the waste-paper basket I have taken public notice of only three. One was that which appeared in the Scots Observer. I noticed it because it made a suggestion, about the intention of the author in writing the book, which needed correction. The second was an article in the St. James's Gazette. It was offensively and vulgarly written, and seemed to me to require immediate and caustic censure. The tone of the article was an impertinence to any man of letters.

The third was a meek attack in a paper called the Daily Chronicle. I think my writing to the Daily Chronicle was an act of pure wilfulness. In fact, I feel sure it was. I quite forget what they said. I believe they said that "Dorian Gray" was poisonous, and I thought that, on alliterative grounds, it would be kind to remind them that, however that may be, it is at any rate perfect. That was all. Of the other two hundred and thirteen criticisms I have taken no notice. Indeed, I have not read more than half of them. It is a sad thing, but one wearies even of praise.

As regards Mr. Brown's letter, it is interesting only in so far as it exemplifies the truth of what I have said above on the question of the two obvious schools of critics. Mr. Brown says frankly that he considers morality to be the "strong point" of my story. Mr. Brown means well, and has got hold of a half truth, but when he proceeds to deal with the book from the artistic stand-point, he, of course, goes sadly astray. To class "Dorian Gray" with M. Zola's La Terre is as silly as if one were to class Masset's Fortunio with one of the Adelphi melodramas. Mr. Brown should be content with ethical appreciations. There he is impregnable.

Mr. Cobbam opens badly by describing my letter setting Mr. Whibley right on a matter of fact as an "impudent paradox." The term "impudent" is meaningless, and the word "paradox" is misplaced. I am afraid that writing to newspapers has a deteriorating influence on style. People get violent and abusive and lose all sense of proportion when they enter that curious journalistic arena in which the race is always to the noisiest. "Impudent paradox" is neither violent not abusive, but it is not an expression that should have been used about my letter.

However, Mr. Cobbam makes full atonement afterwards for what was, no doubt, a mere error of manner, by adopting the impudent paradox in question as his own, and pointing out that, as I had previously said, the artist will always look at the work of art from the stand-point of beauty of style and beauty of treatment, and that those who have not got the sense of beauty, or whose sense of beauty is dominated by ethical considerations, will always turn their attention to the subject-matter and make its moral import the test and touchstone of the poem or novel or picture that is presented to them, while the newspaper critic will sometimes take one side and sometimes the other, according as he is cultured or uncultured. In fact, Mr. Cobbam converts the impudent paradox into a tedious truism, and, I dare say, in doing so does good service.

The English public likes tediousness, and likes things to be explained to it in a tedious way.

Mr. Cobbam has, I have no doubt, already repented of the unfortunate expression with which he has made his début, so I will say no more about it. As far as I am concerned he is quite forgiven.

And finally, Sir, in taking leave of the Scots Observer, I feel bound to make a candid confession to you.

It has been suggested to me by a great friend of mine, who is a charming and distinguished man of letters (and not unknown to you personally), that there have been really only two people engaged in this terrible controversy, and that those two people are the editor of the Scots Observer and the author of "Dorian Gray."

At dinner this evening, over some excellent Chianti, my friend insisted that under assumed and mysterious names you had simply given dramatic expression to the views of some of the semi-educated classes of our community, and that the letters signed "H." were your own skilful, if somewhat bitter caricature of the Philistine as drawn by himself. I admit that something of the kind had occurred to me when I read "H.'s" first letter, the one in which he proposed that the test of art should be the political opinions of the artist, and that if one differed from the artist on the question of the best way of mis-governing Ireland, one should always abuse his work. Still, there are such infinite varieties of Philistines, and North Britain is so renowned for seriousness, that I dismissed the idea as unworthy of the editor of a Scotch paper. I now fear that I was wrong, and that you have been amusing yourself all the time by inventing little puppets and teaching them how to use big words. Well, Sir, if it be so and my friend is strong on the point, allow me to congratulate you most sincerely on the cleverness with which you have reproduced the lack of literary style which is, I am told, essential for any dramatic and life-like characterisation. I confess that I was completely taken in; but I bear no malice; and as you have, no doubt, been laughing at me up your sleeve, let me join openly in the laugh, though it be a little against myself. A comedy ends when the secret is out. Drop your curtain and put your dolls to bed. I love Don Quixote, but I do not wish to fight any longer with marionettes, however cunning may be the master-hand that works their wires. Let them go, Sir, on the shelf. The shelf is the proper place for them. On some future occasion you can re-label them and bring them out for amusement. They are an excellent company, and go well through their tricks, and if they are a little unreal I am not the one to object to unreality in art. The jest is really a good one. The only thing that I cannot understand is why you gave the marionettes such extraordinary and improbable names.

I remain, Sir, your obedient servant,

OSCAR WILDE.

The correspondence continued for three weeks longer, but Oscar Wilde took
no further part in it.

[17] August 16th.

If a man's work is easy to understand an explanation is unnecessary, and if
his work is incomprehensible an explanation is wicked.

PROFUSE AND PERFERVID.

The review in The Speaker[18] which Oscar Wilde referred to in his letter
to The Scots Observer (see par. above starting with: 'And so in the case of
"Dorian Gray,"'), was as follows:

By a stroke of good fortune, singular at this season the two stories[19]
which we have taken up to review this week turn out to be, each in its way,
of no slight interest. Of Mr. Wilde's work, this was to be expected. Let it
be granted, to begin with, that the conception of the story is exceedingly
strong.

A young man of remarkable beauty, perfect in body, but undeveloped, or
rather, lacking altogether, in soul, becomes the dear friend of a painter
of genius. The artist under the spell of this friendship, is painting the
youth's portrait. Enter to them the spirit of evil, in the shape of Lord
Henry Wotton, an extremely "fin de siècle" gentleman, who, by a few
inspiring words, supplies, or calls into life, the boy's missing soul, and
it is an evil one. Henceforward, the tale develops the growth of this evil
soul, side by side with this mystery, that while vice and debauchery write
no wrinkle on the boy's face, but pass from it as a breath off a pane,
every vile action scores its mark upon the portrait, which keeps accurate
record of a loathsome life.

It has been insinuated that this story should be suppressed in the interest
of morality. Mr. Wilde has answered that art and ethics have nothing to do
with each other. His boldness in resting his defence on the general
proposition is the more exemplary, as he might fairly have insisted on the
particular proposition, that the teaching of the book is conspicuously
right in morality. If we have correctly interpreted the book's motive and
we are at a loss to conceive what other can be devised, this position is
unassailable. There is, perhaps, a passage or so in the description of
Dorian's decline that were better omitted. But this is a matter of taste.

The motive of the tale, then, is strong. It is in his treatment of it that
Mr. Wilde has failed, and his mistakes are easy of detection. Whether they
can be as readily corrected is doubtful. To begin with, the author has a
style as striking as his matter; but he has entirely missed reconciling the
two. There is an amateurish lack of precision in the descriptive passages.
They are laboured, finikin, overlaid with paint; and, therefore, they want
vigour. "The Picture of Dorian Gray," has been compared, very naturally,
with "Dr. Jekyll and Mr. Hyde" and we would invite Mr. Wilde to take up
that story, and consider the bold, sharply defined strokes with which its
atmosphere and "milieu" are put in. Such brevity as Mr. Stevenson's comes
from sureness of knowledge, not want of care, and is the first sign of
mastery. Nor is Mr. Wilde too wordy alone; he is too paradoxical. Only the
cook who has yet to learn will run riot in truffles, We will admit at once
that Lord Henry's epigrams are admirable examples, taken separately; but a

story demands simplicity and proportion, and here we have neither; it demands restraint, and here we find profusion only; it demands point, and here the point is too often obscured by mere cleverness. Lord Henry's mission in the book is to lead Dorian Gray to destruction; and he does so, if you please, at the end of a string of epigrams.

In fact we should doubt that Mr. Wilde possessed the true story teller's temperament were it not for some half a dozen passages. Here is one where, Dorian tells of his engagement to Sibyl Vane, the actress:

"Lips," he says, "that Shakespeare taught to speak have whispered their secret in my ear. I have had the arms of Rosalind around me, and kissed Juliet on the mouth."

"Yes, Dorian, I suppose you were right," said Hallward slowly.

"Have you seen her to-day?" said Lord Henry.

Dorian Gray shook his head. "I left her in the forest of Arden, I shall find her in an orchard in Verona."

Lord Henry sipped his champagne in a meditative manner. "At what particular point did you mention the word marriage, Dorian? and what did she say in answer? Perhaps you forgot all about it."

"My dear Harry, I did not treat it as a business transaction, and I did not make any formal proposal. I told her that I loved her, and she said she was not worthy to be my wife. Not worthy! why, the whole world is nothing to me compared to her."

"Women are wonderfully practical," murmured Lord Henry, "much more practical than we are....[20]"

The last chapter of the tale is good story telling throughout, in style and matter, as good as Chapter IX is bad.[21] And when Mr. Wilde thoroughly sees why two particular sentences in that last chapter, "The Park is quite lovely now. I don't think there have been such lilacs since the year I met you," though trivial in themselves are full of significance and beauty in their setting he will be far on the road to eminence in fiction. He has given us a work of serious art, strong and fascinating, in spite of its blemishes. Will he insist on being taken seriously, and go on to give us a better?

[18] Vol. III., No. 27. July 5, 1890.

[19] The second story was "Perfervid: the Career of Ninian Jamieson," by John Davidson (Ward and Downey).

[20] p. 34.

[21] Chapter IX in the Lippincott version is Chapter XI in later editions, the last chapter (XIII) being afterwards divided into two (XIX and XX).

"THE PICTURE OF DORIAN GRAY."

A Spiritualistic Review. By "NIZIDA."

The following review of "Dorian Gray" referred to by Oscar Wilde in his second letter to the Scots Observer (see page 71) was published in the issue of Light dated July 12th, 1890. This is "a Journal of Psychical, Occult, and Mystical Research."

"M.A., Oxon," writing in the same paper a few weeks later mentions that "Oscar Wilde says of Light that it is 'The organ of the English mystics,' and adds 'I do not like that word 'organ.'" At the same time "M.A., Oxon," refers to the Scots Observer as being "bright, wise, witty, and not at all aggressive."

The review is here given in its entirety:

Mr. Oscar Wilde has created a new character in fiction, one likely to absorb public attention with a similar weird fascination to that produced by the renowned Dr. Jekyll and Mr. Hyde; and with a more lasting and beneficial moral effect than had Mr. Stevenson's surprising creation. A deeply conceived psychological study, upon entirely new lines, enriched by the stored wealth of a mind which has spared no pains in the pursuit of sensuous beauty, and which has, to all appearance, revelled in deepest draughts from that sparkling and alluring fountain. But what a spiritual lesson has he drawn therefrom, a lesson graphically and powerfully set forth in the fascinating pages which present to us the life of Dorian Gray. A modern Narcissus, enamoured of his own beauty, which proves a lure to draw him down into the deepest hells of sensual indulgence, from whence he sinks into a still deeper abyss of crime.

Introduced as an innocent, rather effeminate youth of extraordinary and fascinating beauty, Dorian Gray has his eyes opened to the fact that he possesses beauty, and his slumbering vanity and egotism, awakened by the insidious flatteries of a hardened cynic, spring at once into activity, and from that moment begins the downward course. Skilfully the author depicts the budding and gradual unfolding of this baleful life-blossom of the animal soul, seeking only the selfish gratification of the senses, refined indeed by education and artistic culture, but, notwithstanding, purely animal, nay, at times, bestial. By degrees, the still, small voice, the voice of the higher self which spiritually overshadows the unsophisticated youth is deadened in the soul. All the humane, merciful, spiritually beautiful sentiments and emotions of the better nature, are strangled in their infancy, for Dorian Gray drinks so deeply of the intoxicating cup of sensuous gratification, that his nature becomes transformed to that of a demon, beautiful outwardly, but within hideous. All this is depicted with a master hand; the underlying lesson, for those who can find it, being the danger to the soul which lies in an egotistic love and idolatrous cherishing of one's own personal beauty, for male or female equally perilous. But the author by an ingenious device presents to us an objective image of the subjective transformation gradually going on in Dorian Gray's soul, which, for startling vividness and horror, surpasses the effects usually produced by the novelist's art.

Dorian Gray, whilst retaining the youthfulness, vigorous health, and unimpaired beauty of his external form, at the same time witnesses the objective presentment of his soul's growing, loathsome hideousness; and its falling into diseased decrepitude, into an ugliness beyond conception. At first horrified by this, he becomes at length accustomed to it, and at certain stages of his downward course, after the commission of new excesses, he repairs to this silent recorder of his deeds, and unveiling it, seeks for fresh indication of the gradual decay and corruption which are unfailingly represented on this physical side of his being. As time went on

"He grew more and more enamoured of his own beauty, more and more interested in the corruption of his own soul. He would examine with minute

care, and often with a monstrous and terrible delight, the hideous lines
that seared the wrinkling forehead, or crawled around the heavy sensual
mouth, wondering sometimes which were the more horrible, the signs of sins
or the signs of age. He would place his white hands beside the coarse
bloated hands of the picture, and smile. He mocked the misshapen body and
the failing limbs."[22]

Never does he feel a moment of repentance. The disgusting image, however,
haunts him with a terror of discovery, drawing him back from distant places
to assure himself of its hidden security, and to contemplate it with a
hideous fascination. The loathsome horror never departs from his
consciousness. From its veiled seclusion it exerts over him a spell of
diabolical enchantment, and he knows that it is he himself; but his mirror
presents to his gaze the personal beauty he cherishes, and the world
continues to be fascinated by his charm. Many become fascinated to their
serious moral and spiritual injury. His victims are numerous; innocent
women and upright young men, who, but for him, would have led virtuous,
useful lives. With his beautiful body, cared for as one would care for some
rare exotic blossom, going about the world with a charming appearance of
harmlessness and even innocence, he murdered souls in secret, as completely
as if with his slender, white, taper fingers he might have clutched their
throats and strangled the life out of their bodies.

And all this rottenness, all this corruption, had been proximately caused
by a seed dropped into a soil prepared for it, the soul left doubtless from
the Karma of some previous life. A seed dropped from the flattering tongue
of Lord Henry Wotton, tended and skilfully fostered into a surprising
precociousness by his insidious, worthless cynicisms, and oracular
sophistries. A man out of whose life had departed every wholesome savour,
who poisoned the lives of others, and led them to sin, whilst, apparently,
he sinned not himself. As a friend once said to him, "You never say a moral
thing, and you never do a wrong thing. Your cynicism is simply a pose." His
whole life was, however, a sin, concealed behind a mask of bonhommie, a
fashionable cheerfulness and pleasantness of manner; a hollow cadavre full
of the dust and ashes of a burnt-out life. One of Lord Henry Wotton's
specious sophistries was this: "The only way to get rid of a temptation is
to yield to it." As well wrap oneself confidingly in the folds of a boa-
constrictor, hoping to save one's life thereby. Lord Henry's apt pupil,
Dorian Gray, followed this advice scrupulously, only to increase the power
of temptation, which never after found him unwilling, until at last all of
his higher nature was suffocated. The author skilfully depicts the
insidious, baleful influence of Lord Henry Wotton, but attributes the
corruption of Dorian Gray's soul to a book which Lord Henry loaned him. He
says:

"The Renaissance knew of strange manners of poisoning, poisoning by a
helmet, and a lighted torch, by an embroidered glove, and a jewelled fan,
by a gilded pomander, and by an amber chain. Dorian Gray was poisoned by a
book. There were moments when he looked on evil simply as a mode through
which he could realise his conception of the beautiful."[23]

Dorian Gray had conceived the idea that his life was the product of many
preceding lives. The author causes him to make the following reflections:

"He used to wonder at the shallow psychology of those who conceive the Ego
in man as a thing simple, permanent, reliable, and of one essence. To him,
man was a being with myriad lives and myriad sensations, a complex
multiform creature that bore within itself strange legacies of thought and
passion, and whose very flesh was tainted with the monstrous maladies of
the dead. He loved to stroll through the gaunt cold picture-gallery of his
country house and look at the various portraits of those whose blood flowed

in his veins. Here was Philip Herbert, described by Francis Osborne in his Memoirs on the Reigns of Queen Elizabeth and King James as one who was "caressed by the Court for his handsome face, which kept him not long company." Was it young Herbert's life that he sometimes led? Had some strange poisonous germ crept from body to body till it had reached his own? Was it some dim sense of that ruined grace that had made him so suddenly, and almost without cause, give utterance, in Basil Hallward's studio, to that mad prayer which had so changed his life? Here in gold embroidered red doublet, jewelled sur-coat, and gilt edged ruff and wrist-bands, stood Sir Anthony Sherard, with his silver and black armour piled at his feet. What had this man's legacy been? Had the lover of Giovanni of Naples bequeathed him some inheritance of sins and shame? Were his own actions merely the dreams that the dead man had not dared to realise? Here, from the fading canvas smiled Lady Elizabeth Devereux, in her gauze hood, pearled stomacher, and pink slashed sleeves. A flower was in her right hand, and her left clasped an enamelled collar of white and damask roses. On a table by her side lay a mandolin and an apple. There were large green rosettes upon her little pointed shoes. He knew her life, and the strange stories that were told about her lovers. Had he something of her temperament in him? Those oval heavy-lidded eyes seemed to look curiously at him. What of George Willoughby, with his powdered hair and fantastic patches? How evil he looked! The face was saturnine and swarthy, and the sensual lips seemed to be twisted with disdain. Delicate lace ruffles fell over the lean yellow hands that were so overladen with rings. He had been a macaroni of the eighteenth century, and the friend, in his youth, of Lord Ferrars. What of the second Lord Sherard, the companion of the Prince Regent in his wildest days, and one of the witnesses of the secret marriage with Mrs. Fitzherbert? How proud and handsome he was, with his chestnut curls and insolent pose! What passions had he bequeathed? The world had looked upon him as infamous. He had led the orgies at Carlton House. The Star of the Garter glittered upon his breast. Beside him hung the portrait of his wife, a pallid, thin-lipped woman in black. Her blood also stirred within him. How curious it all seemed!"[24]

What a pity Dorian did not see that the sole reason for a plurality of lives was that very thirst of the animal soul for the sensual pleasures of the material life in which he so wildly indulged, and yet with a diabolical, smooth, and easy method in his madness, seeking ever the externally beautiful. Beauty fled indeed before the gaunt ugliness of crime; but when this happened to Dorian, he coolly turned his back and went in search of new sensations.

"And in his search for sensations that would be at once new and delightful and possess that element of strangeness that is so essential to romance, he would often adopt certain modes of thought that he knew to be really alien to his nature, abandon himself to their subtle influences, and then, having, as it were, caught their colour and satisfied his intellectual curiosity, leave them with that curious indifference that is not incompatible with a real ardour of temperament, and that, indeed, according to certain modern psychologists, is often a condition of it."[25]

Veil it as he would, his extreme moral corruption became known, crept out from behind skilful concealments, and was borne by the breath of gossip and scandal, whispering of its enormities. He was black-balled in a West End Club,

"and when brought by a friend into a smoking-room of the Carlton, the Duke of Berwick and another gentleman got up in a marked manner and went out. Curious stories became current about him after he had passed his twenty-fifth year. ... Men would whisper to each other in corners, or pass him with a sneer, or look at him with cold, searching eyes. Of such insolences and attempted slights, he, of course, took no notice; and in the opinion of most people his frank manner, his charming, boyish smile, and the infinite grace of that wonderful youth that seemed never to leave him were in themselves a sufficient answer to the calumnies (for so they called them) that were circulated about him."[26]

The life at length culminates in the commission of a crime of the most cruel, treacherous, and dastardly character. It is successfully concealed. The extraordinary coolness, even peace of mind, which Dorian experiences after this deed of horror is powerfully depicted. But he does feel a few momentary, weak qualms of conscience. He spares one of his victims, and he thinks of beginning a new life. Then imagining himself becoming purified he longs to see how his silent recorder looks. He expects to find some wonderful improvement in the aspect of the loathsome hidden self he has created, so he repairs to its hiding place. It is more loathsome than ever, and presents new aspects of ugliness. In a moment of supreme disgust and aversion he seizes a knife to destroy it. By so doing he ends his physical life.

The only occult explanation of the catastrophe which befalls him is, that he commits astral suicide by the murderous attack he ignorantly makes upon that which represented to him his own soul. The blow reverts to his physical body, and he falls dead.

There is in this book a wonderful spiritual insight into the inner life of the human being. Arising, in all probability from that intuition we all more or less possess; a sort of flash of truth upon the mind, which is not known at the moment to be really true, but is supposed to be the mere weaving of a graceful prolific fancy. A similar power lay at the back of Mr. R. Stevenson's creation of Dr. Jekyll, casting upon the tale so powerful a spiritual light, that all readers were held by the spell of its enchantment. The same feeling of being under a spell fills the reader of "The Picture of Dorian Gray." The same subtle, spiritual effect of the aura of evil flows out from the book, especially at those moments when Dorian is contemplating the image of his soul's corruption, not, in this instance, that the evil so powerfully felt poisons the mind as poor Dorian was poisoned for life by his French novel; but one gets a feeling of painful horror, and sickening disgust, it is not easy to shake off. One seems to have glanced momentarily into the deepest abysses of hell, and to have drawn back totally sickened by a subtle effluvium. This singular power possessed by both these writers reveals a certain growth or development in them of the spiritual nature, which need not necessarily, as yet, convert either of these gentlemen into saints, or angels, although doubtless they are both very good Men.

The lesson taught by Mr. Oscar Wilde's powerful story is of the highest spiritual import; and if it can be, not believed merely, but accepted as a literal fact, a mysterious verity in the life of a human being, that the invisible soul within the body, that alone which lives after death, is deformed, bestialised, and even murdered by a life of persistent evil, it ought to have the most beneficial effect upon society.

Let him depict the soul as he may, except in the case of Basil Hallward, Mr. Wilde never rises above the animal soul in man. It is the animal soul alone, dominated by a refined but perverted intellect, seeking an animal gratification in sensuous beauty, which he puts before us. Dorian Gray suffocated in its infancy the only germ of spiritual soul he possessed.

[22] Pp. 65, 66.
[23] p. 77.
[24] p. 75.

[25] p. 68.
[26] p. 74.

The fact of a man being a poisoner is nothing against his prose.

PARALLEL. Joe, the Fat Boy in Pickwick, startles the Old Lady; Oscar, the Fad Boy in Lippincott's, startles Mrs. Grundy: Oscar, the Fad Boy: "I want to make your flesh creep!"

Reproduced by special permission of the proprietors of "Punch."

PUNCH on "DORIAN GRAY."

By special permission of the Proprietors of Punch the following review is reproduced from the issue of that journal dated July 19th, 1890.

OUR BOOKING OFFICE.

The Baron has read Oscar Wilde's wildest and Oscarest work, called "Dorian Gray," a weird sensational romance, complete in one number of Lippincott's Magazine. The Baron recommends anybody who revels in diablerie, to begin it about half-past ten, and to finish it at one sitting up; but those who do not so revel he advises either not to read it at all, or to choose the daytime, and take it in homoeopathic doses.

The portrait represents the soul of the beautiful Ganymede-like Dorian Gray, whose youth and beauty last to the end, while his soul, like John Brown's, "goes marching on," into the Wilderness of Sin. It becomes at last a devilled soul. And then Dorian sticks a knife into it, as any ordinary mortal might do, and a fork also, and next morning

"Lifeless but 'hideous,' he lay," while the portrait has recovered the perfect beauty which it possessed when it first left the artist's easel.

If Oscar intended an allegory, the finish is dreadfully wrong. Does he mean that, by sacrificing his earthly life, Dorian Gray atones for his infernal sins, and so purifies his soul by suicide? "Heavens! I am no preacher," says the Baron, "and perhaps Oscar didn't mean anything at all, except to give us a sensation, to show how like Bulwer Lytton's old-world style he could make his descriptions and his dialogue, and what an easy thing it is to frighten the respectable Mrs. Grundy with a Bogie." The style is decidedly Lyttonerary. His aphorisms are Wilde, yet forced. Mr. Oscar Wilde says of his story, "it is poisonous if you like, but you cannot deny that it is also perfect, and perfection is what we artists aim at."[27] Perhaps, but "we artists" do not always hit what we aim at, and despite his confident claim to unerring marksmanship, one must hazard the opinion, that in this case Mr. Wilde has "shot wide." There is indeed more of "poison" than of "perfection" in "Dorian Gray."

The central idea is an excellent, if not exactly a novel, one; and a finer art, say that of Nathaniel Hawthorne, would have made a striking and satisfying story of it. "Dorian Gray" is striking enough, in a sense, but it is not "satisfying" artistically, any more than it is so ethically. Mr. Wilde has preferred the senuous and hyperdecorative manner of "Mademoiselle de Maupin," and without Gautier's power, has spoilt a promising conception by clumsy unideal treatment.

His "decoration" (upon which he plumes himself) is indeed "laid on with a trowel." The luxuriously elaborate details of his "artistic hedonism," are too suggestive of South Kensington Museum and æsthetic Encyclopædias. A truer art would have avoided both the glittering conceits, which bedeck the body of the story, and the unsavoury suggestiveness which lurks in its spirit.

Poisonous! Yes. But the loathly "leperous distilment" taints and spoils, without in any way subserving "perfection," artistic or otherwise. If Mrs. Grundy doesn't read it, the younger Grundies do; that is, the Grundies who belong to Clubs, and who care to shine in certain sets wherein this story will be much discussed. "I have read it, and, except for the ingenious idea, I wish to forget it," says the Baron.

[27] See letter to Daily Chronicle page 61.

The note of doom that like a purple thread runs through the texture of "Dorian Gray."

A REVULSION FROM REALISM. [28]

By ANNE H. WHARTON.

In all ages and climes mankind has found delight in romances based upon the mystic, the improbable and the impossible, from the days when the Norse poets sang their Sagas through long Northern nights, and the fair Scheherezade, under Southern moon, charmed her bloodthirsty lord by her tales of wonder, to our own day, when Stevenson and Crawford and Haggard hold fancy spellbound by their entirely improbable stories. Scott and Bulwer played with master hands upon the love of the mysterious and supernatural inherent in mankind; Dickens and others have essayed to gratify its demands, but with less daring, and, having an eye always on the moorings of the actual, their success has been less marked. With the elder Hawthorne such romance-writing seemed the natural growth of an exquisitely sensitive and spiritual nature, while among later French writers Théophile Gautier and Edmond About have entered into the domain of the impossible as into the natural heritage of their genius, sporting in its impalpable ether with the tuneful abandon of a fish in the sea, or a bird in the air, hampered by no bond of the actual, weighted by no encumbrance of the material.

It is not strange that the great influx of realistic novels that has flowed in upon the last decade should be followed by a revulsion to the impossible in fiction. Men and women, wearied with meeting the same characters and events in so-called romance that they encounter in every-day life, or saddened by the depressing, if dramatic, pictures of Tolstoi and the cool vivisection of humanity presented by Ibsen, turn with a sense of rest and refreshment to the guidance of those who, like Robert Louis Stevenson and Rider Haggard, lead them suddenly into the mystic land of wonder, or, like Marion Crawford and Mrs. Oliphant, delight to draw them, by gentle and easy stages, from the midst of a well-appointed setting of every-day life into the shadowy borderland that lies between the real and the unreal. Much of the success of such romance writing rests upon the rebound, natural to humanity, from intense realism to extreme ideality; more, perhaps, upon the fact that this age which is grossly material is also deeply spiritual. With these two facts well in view, Mr. Oscar Wilde has fallen into line, and entered the lists with some of the most successful masters of fiction. In his novel "The Picture of Dorian Gray," written for the July Lippincott's,

Mr. Wilde, like Balzac and the authors of "Faust" and "John Inglesant," presents to us the drama of a human soul, while, like Gautier and About, he surrounds his utterly impossible story with a richness and depth of colouring and a grace and airiness of expression that make the perusal of its pages an artistic delight.

If Mr. Wilde's romance resembles the productions of some of the writers of the French school in its reality and tone, it still more strongly resembles Mr. Stevenson's most powerfully wrought fairy tale, "Dr. Jekyll and Mr. Hyde," although the moral of the story is brought out even more plainly, as plainly, indeed, as in the drama of "Faust." In both Mr. Stevenson's and Mr. Wilde's stories there is a transformation or substitution. In one the soul of Dr. Jekyll appears under different exteriors; in the other some fine influence passes from the soul of Dorian Gray into his portrait and there works a gradual and subtle change upon the pictured lineaments. Although. Mr. Wilde's extravaganza is far less dramatic than that of Mr. Stevenson, it has the advantage of richer colouring and a more human setting, if we may so express it. The characters in "The Picture of Dorian Gray," enjoy life more than Mr. Stevenson's creations, who seem to have had so dull a time of it at the best that they might have been expected to welcome a tragedy, as a relief to the tedium of their daily lives. Mr. Utterson, we are told, was good but he was evidently not particularly happy,[29] which was the case with the other personages of the drama, with the exception of those who were signally wretched. On the other hand, Mr. Wilde's characters are happy during their little day. Their world is a luxurious, perfumed land of delight, until sin transforms it, and, even after Lord Henry has corrupted the nature of Dorian Gray with evil books and worldly philosophy, he occasionally drinks of the waters of Lethe and enjoys some fragments of what may be called happiness, while Lord Henry himself seems to derive a certain satisfaction from the practice of his Mephistophelian art and in his entire freedom from the restraints of conscience. In a tale of the impossible it is not required that the writer should be true to life, animate or inanimate, yet in the fact that there are glimpses of light through the clouds that surround his dramatis personæ, that they inhabit a world in which the laburnum hangs out yellow clusters in June, and the clematis robes itself with purple stars, and the sun sheds gold and the moon silver, despite the tragedy that touches the lives of its inhabitants, is not Mr. Wilde quite as true to nature as to art?

The reader may reasonably question the author's good taste in displaying at such length his knowledge of antique decoration and old-world crime as in Chapter IX,[30] which, besides being somewhat tiresome, clogs the dramatic movement of the story. Yet, on the other hand, it must be admitted that none but an artist and an apostle of the beautiful could have so sympathetically portrayed the glowing hues and perfumes of the garden in which Dorian Gray had first presented to his lips the cup of life, and none other could have so pictured the luxurious surroundings of his home, for whose embellishment the known world had been searched for hangings, ornaments and bric-à-brac. Amid such an entourage of modern London life, with its Sybaritic indulgence, its keenness of wit and its subtle intelligence, Mr. Wilde places his characters and works out his miracle.

Viewing his own portrait, just completed by an artist friend, Dorian Gray turns from it filled with envy and dissatisfaction, because it has been whispered in his ear that youth is the supreme possession in life, and that when youth and beauty have fled from his face and form this pictured presentment will live forever, a perpetual mockery of himself, whom withering age has overtaken. Under the influence of his evil genius, Lord Henry Wotton, Dorian Gray utters a prayer that he may always remain young, and the portrait alone reveal the ravages of time, sin and sorrow. The

realization of this idea is the theory of Mr. Wilde's romance, and the air
of probability with which he has endowed the absolutely impossible
evidences the artistic and dramatic power of the writer. The portrait of
Dorian Gray, painted in days of innocence and loveliness, when his mere
presence symbolized to the artist the entire harmony between beauty of body
and beauty of soul, changes day by day with the degradation of his nature,
while the living Dorian Gray, after years of sin, remorseless cruelty and
corruption of thought and action, preserves all the grace and fairness of
his Antinous-like youth.

Love in this romance is an incident, not its crowning event, although an
important incident as a revelation of the character of Dorian Gray. The
reader never meets Sybil Vane; he merely sees her on the stage and hears of
her from the lips of her lover; yet even thus she appeals to us as an
exquisite personation of maidenhood with all its purity and all its
tenderness. As shadowy an outline as the fair child whom Bulwer allows to
captivate the imagination of Kenelm Chillingly, who caught butterflies,
talked philosophy and died young, yet who in her brief transit across his
path realized to his poetic soul all the best possibilities of life,
spiritual and material, Sibyl Vane comes to us girt about with ideal charm,
to fulfil her widely different mission, which was to reveal to Dorian Gray
the sad fact that his soul had passed beyond her sweet and ennobling
influence. His artistic and intellectual senses were touched by her beauty
and dramatic power, but to the beauty that made her worthy to be loved, his
eyes were blind, his heart was insensible. The tragedy of the story, the
climax of the situation, is not the death of Sybil Vane, nor even the
pitiless murder of the friend who dared to give Dorian Gray good counsel,
but the disclosure that Dorian's soul, once open to all good influences,
had, by yielding to the malign domination of his evil genius, passed beyond
the reach of love, pity or remorse.

It is needless to say that Dorian Gray is not a very substantial character.
The most entertaining, though not the most exemplary, personage of the
story is Lord Henry Wotton, who by his preaching and practice of the
doctrine of hedonism leads Dorian Gray into all known and unknown evil,
until finally his darkling shadow outreaches in depravity the imagination
of his tempter. When his victim has sunk so low in sin that the world shuns
him, Lord Henry still enjoys his gay, conscienceless existence, and
continues to utter the persiflage that constitutes much of the attraction
of the book as well of his society. Debonair, witty, learned, giving
expression to aphorisms as keen as the sayings of Thackeray's characters,
with the moral element eliminated, and as cynical as those of Norris, with
exquisite taste and the fascination of a finished man of the world, Lord
Henry belongs as truly, on the material side of his nature, to the life of
to-day, as he appertains on its spiritual side to the region of Pluto. A
gay child of the great London social world, he hovers airily around and
about the emotions of life, declaring that death is the only thing that
ever terrifies him, and that death and vulgarity are the only facts in the
nineteenth century that one cannot explain away. The climax of Lord Henry's
sardonic worldliness is reached when he becomes the spectator of his own
domesticity, if he may be said to have any, and speaks to Dorian of his
divorce from his wife as one of the latest sensations of London, remarking
apropos of his music, "The man with whom my wife ran away played Chopin
exquisitely. Poor Victoria! I was very fond of her. The house is rather
lonely without her."

Lord Henry is so entirely true to himself and the worst that is in him that
towards the close of the book, when Dorian announces that he is "going to
be good," and begs his friend not to poison another young life with the
book with which he had corrupted his, we find ourselves trembling for
Dorian's one remaining ally, especially when he exclaims, "My dear boy, you

are really beginning to moralize. You will soon be going about warning people against all the sins of which you have grown tired. You are much too delightful to do that. Besides, it is no use. You and I are what we are, and we will be what we will be." Had not the hero stabbed himself, or his picture (which was it?) it is only a question of time how soon Dorian Gray, with the slightest obtrusion of conscience, would have ceased to charm him who had welcomed him as a débutant on the Stage of Pleasure, where, to use his favourite saying, "the only way to get rid of a temptation is to yield to it." Dorian Gray struggling against the temptations of the world would have proved an inartistic and disturbing element in the life of Lord Henry.

All that is needed to complete the tale is Lord Henry's own comment on the highly dramatic taking-off of his friend. This chapter, Mr. Wilde, true to his artistic instinct, has not finished, preferring to leave appetite unappeased, rather than to create satiety by making his Mephistopheles say precisely what one would expect him to say under the circumstances.

[28] Lippincott's Monthly Magazine, September, 1890.

[29] "When we are happy we are always good, but when we are good we are not always happy." DORIAN GRAY, chap. vi. (Ed.)

[30] Chapter XI. in the 1891 edition.

THE ROMANCE OF THE IMPOSSIBLE.

By JULIAN HAWTHORNE.[31]

Fiction which flies at all game, has latterly taken to the Impossible as its quarry. The pursuit is interesting and edifying, if one goes properly equipped, and with adequate skill. But if due care is not exercised, the impossible turns upon the hunter and grinds him to powder. It is a very dangerous and treacherous kind of wild-fowl. The conditions of its existence, if existence can be predicated on that which does not exist, are so peculiar and abstruse that only genius is really capable of taming it and leading it captive. But the capture, when it is made, is so delightful and fascinating that every tyro would like to try. One is reminded of the princess of the fairy-tale, who was to be won on certain preposterous terms, and if the terms were not met, the discomfited suitor lost his head. Many misguided or over-weening youths perished; at last the One succeeded. Failure in a romance of the Impossible is apt to be a disastrous failure; on the other hand, success carries great rewards.

Of course, the idea is not a new one. The writings of the alchemists are stories of the Impossible. The fashion has never been entirely extinct. Balzac wrote the "Peau de Chagrin," and probably this tale is as good a one as was ever written of that kind. The possessor of the Skin may have everything he wishes for; but each wish causes the Skin to shrink, and when it is all gone the wisher is annihilated with it. By the art of the writer this impossible thing is made to appear quite feasible; by touching the chords of coincidence and fatality, the reader's common-sense is soothed to sleep. We feel that all this might be, and yet no natural law be violated; and yet we know that such a thing never was and never will be. But the vitality of the story, as of all good stories of the sort, is due to the fact that it is the symbol of a spiritual verity: the life of indulgence, the selfish life, destroys the soul. This psychic truth is so deeply felt that its sensible embodiment is rendered plausible. In the case of another famous romance, "Frankenstein", the technical art is entirely wanting: a worse story from the literary point of view has seldom been written. But the soul of it, so to speak, is so potent and obvious that, although no one actually reads the book nowadays, everybody knows the gist of the idea. "Frankenstein" has entered into the language, for it utters a perpetual truth of human nature.

At the present moment the most conspicuous success in the line we are considering is Stevenson's "Dr. Jekyll and Mr. Hyde." The author's literary skill, in that awful little parable, is at its best, and makes the most of every point. To my thinking, it is an artistic mistake to describe Hyde's transformation as actually taking place in plain sight of the audience; the sense of spiritual mystery is thereby lost, and a mere brute miracle takes its place. But the tale is strong enough to carry this imperfection, and the moral significance of it is so catholic, it so comes home to every soul that considers it, that it has already made an ineffaceable impression on the public mind. Every man is his own Jekyll and Hyde, only without the magic powder. On the bookshelf of the Impossible, Mr. Stevenson's book may take its place beside Balzac's.

Mr. Oscar Wilde, the apostle of beauty, has in the July number of Lippincott's Magazine, a novel, or romance (it partakes of the qualities of both), which everybody will want to read. It is a story strange in conception, strong in interest, and fitted with a tragic and ghastly climax. Like many stories of its class, it is open to more than one interpretation; and there are, doubtless, critics who will deny that it has any meaning at all. It is, at all events, a salutary departure from the ordinary English novel, with the hero and heroine of different social stations, the predatory black sheep, the curate, the settlements and Society. Mr. Wilde, as we all know, is a gentleman of an original and audacious turn of mind, and the commonplace is scarcely possible to him. Besides, his advocacy of novel ideas in life, art, dress and demeanour had led us to expect surprising things from him; and in this literary age it is agreed that a man may best show the best there is in him by writing a book. Those who read Mr. Wilde's story in the hope of finding in it some compact and final statement of his theories of life and manners will be satisfied in some respects, and dissatisfied in others; but not many will deny that the book is a remarkable one and would attract attention even had it appeared without the author's name on the title-page.

"The Picture of Dorian Gray," begins to show its quality in the opening pages. Mr. Wilde's writing has what is called "colour," the quality that forms the mainstay of many of Ouida's works, and it appears in the sensuous descriptions of nature and of the decorations and environments of the artistic life. The general aspect of the characters and the tenor of their conversation remind one a little of "Vivian Gray" and a little of "Pelham," but the resemblance does not go far: Mr. Wilde's objects and philosophy are different from those of either Disraeli or Bulwer. Meanwhile his talent for aphorisms and epigrams may fairly be compared with theirs: some of his clever sayings are more than clever, they show real insight and a comprehensive grasp. Their wit is generally cynical; but they are put into the mouth of one of the characters, Lord Harry, and Mr. Wilde himself refrains from definitely committing himself to them; though one cannot help suspecting that Mr. Wilde regards Lord Harry as being an uncommonly able fellow. Be that as it may, Lord Harry plays the part of Old Harry in the story, and lives to witness the destruction of every other person in it. He may be taken as an imaginative type of all that is most evil and most refined in modern civilization, a charming, gentle, witty, euphemistic Mephistopheles, who deprecates the vulgarity of goodness, and muses aloud about "those renunciations that men have unwisely called virtue, and those natural rebellions that wise men still call sin." Upon the whole, Lord Harry is the most ably portrayed character in the book, though not the most original in conception. Dorian Gray himself is as nearly a new idea in fiction as one has now-a-days a right to expect. If he had been adequately realized and worked out, Mr. Wilde's first novel would have been remembered after more meritorious ones were forgotten. But, even as "nemo repente fuit turpissimus," so no one, or hardly any one, creates a thoroughly original figure at a first essay. Dorian never quite solidifies. In fact, his portrait is rather the more real thing of the two. But this needs explanation.

The story consists of a strong and marvellous central idea, illustrated by three characters, all men. There are a few women in the background, but they are only mentioned: they never appear to speak for themselves. There is, too, a valet who brings in his master's breakfasts, and a chemist who by some scientific miracle, disposes of a human body: but, substantially, the book is taken up with the artist who paints the portrait, with his friend Lord Harry aforesaid, and with Dorian Gray, who might, so far as the story goes, stand alone. He and his portrait are one, and their union points the moral of the tale.

The situation is as follows. Dorian Gray is a youth of extraordinary physical beauty and grace, and pure and innocent of soul. An artist sees him and falls æsthetically in love with him, and finds in him a new inspiration in his art, both direct and general. In the lines of his form and features, and in his colouring and movement, are revealed fresh and profound laws: he paints him in all guises and combinations, and it is seen and admitted on all sides that he has never before painted so well. At length he concentrates all his knowledge and power in a final portrait, which has the vividness and grace of life itself, and, considering how much both of the sitter and of the painter is embodied in it, might almost be said to live. The portrait is declared by Lord Harry to be the greatest work of modern art; and he himself thinks so well of it that he resolves never to exhibit it, even as he would shrink from exposing to public gaze the privacies of his own nature.

On the day of the last sitting a singular incident occurs. Lord Harry, meeting with Dorian Gray for the first time, is no less impressed than was Hallward, the artist, with the youth's radiant beauty and freshness. But whereas Hallward would keep Dorian unspotted from the world, and would have him resist evil temptations and all the allurements of corruption, Lord Harry, on the contrary, with a truly Satanic ingenuity, discourses to the young man on the matchless delights and privileges of youth. Youth is the golden period of life: youth comes never again: in youth only are the senses endowed with divine potency; only then are joys exquisite and pleasures unalloyed. Let it therefore be indulged without stint. Let no harsh and cowardly restraints be placed upon its glorious impulses. Men are virtuous through fear and selfishness. They are too dull or too timid to take advantage of the godlike gifts that are showered upon them in the morning of existence; and before they can realise the folly of their self-denial, the morning has passed, and weary day is upon them, and the shadows of night are near. But let Dorian, who is matchless in the vigour and resources of his beauty, rise above the base shrinking from life that calls itself goodness. Let him accept and welcome every natural impulse of his nature. The tragedy of old age is not that one is old, but that one is young: let him so live that when old age comes he shall at least have the satisfaction of knowing that no opportunity of pleasure and indulgence has escaped untasted.

This seductive sermon profoundly affects the innocent Dorian, and he looks at life and himself with new eyes. He realizes the value as well as the transitoriness of that youth and beauty which hitherto he had accepted as a matter of course and as a permanent possession. Gazing on his portrait, he laments that it possesses the immortality of loveliness and comeliness that is denied to him; and, in a sort of imaginative despair, he utters a wild

prayer that to the portrait, and not to himself, may come the feebleness
and hideousness of old age; that whatever sins he may commit, to whatever
indulgences he may surrender himself, not upon him but upon the portrait
may the penalties and disfigurements fall. Such is Dorian's prayer; and,
though at first he suspects it not, his prayer is granted. From that hour,
the evil of his life is registered upon the face and form of his pictured
presentment, while he himself goes unscathed. Day by day, each fresh sin
that he commits stamps its mark of degradation upon the painted image.
Cruelty sensuality, treachery, all nameless crimes, corrupt and render
hideous the effigy on the canvas; he sees in it the gradual pollution and
ruin of his soul, while his own fleshly features preserve unstained all the
freshness and virginity of his sinless youth. The contrast at first alarms
and horrifies him; but at length he becomes accustomed to it, and finds a
sinister delight in watching the progress of the awful change. He locks up
the portrait in a secret chamber, and constantly retires thither to ponder
over the ghastly miracle. No one but he knows or suspects the incredible
truth; and he guards like a murder-secret this visible revelation of the
difference between what he is and what he seems. This is a powerful
situation; and the reader may be left to discover for himself how Mr. Wilde
works it out.

[31] *Lippincott's Monthly Magazine, September, 1890.*

... Pater, who is, on the whole, the most perfect master of English prose
now creating amongst us.

WALTER PATER ON "DORIAN GRAY."

There is always something of an excellent talker about the writing of Mr.
Oscar Wilde, (wrote Pater, in reviewing "Dorian Gray" for The Bookman[32])
and in his hands, as happens so rarely with those who practise it, the form
of dialogue is justified by its being really alive. His genial, laughter-
loving sense of life and its enjoyable intercourse, goes far to obviate any
crudity there may be in the paradox, with which, as with the bright and
shining truth which often underlies it, Mr. Wilde, startling his
"countrymen," carries on, more perhaps than any other writer, the brilliant
critical work of Mathew Arnold. The Decay of Lying, for instance, is all
but unique in its half-humorous, yet wholly convinced, presentment of
certain valuable truths of criticism. Conversational ease, the fluidity of
life, felicitous expression, are qualities which have a natural alliance to
the successful writing of fiction; and side by side with Mr. Wilde's
Intentions (so he entitles his critical efforts) comes a novel, certainly
original, and affording the reader a fair opportunity of comparing his
practice as a creative artist with many a precept he has enounced as critic
concerning it.

A wholesome dislike of the common-place, rightly or wrongly identified by
him with the bourgeois, with our middle-class, its habits and tastes, leads
him to protest emphatically against so-called "realism" in art; life, as he
argues, with much plausibility, as a matter of fact, when it is really
awake, following art, the fashion of an effective artist sets; while art,
on the other hand, influential and effective art, has taken its cue from
actual life. In "Dorian Gray" he is true, certainly, on the whole, to the
æsthetic philosophy of his Intentions; yet not infallibly, even on this
point: there is a certain amount of the intrusion of real life and its
sordid aspects, the low theatre, the pleasures and griefs, the faces of
some very unrefined people, managed, of course, cleverly enough. The
interlude of Jim Vane, his half-sullen but wholly faithful care for his

sister's honour, is as good as perhaps anything of the kind, marked by a homely but real pathos, sufficiently proving a versatility in the writer's talent, which should make his books popular. Clever always, this book, however, seems intended to set forth anything but a homely philosophy of life for the middle-class, a kind of dainty Epicurean theory, rather yet fails, to some degree in this; and one can see why. A true Epicureanism aims at a complete though harmonious development of man's entire organism. To lose the moral sense therefore, for instance, the sense of sin and righteousness, as Mr. Wilde's hero, his heroes are bent on doing as speedily, as completely as they can, is to lose, or lower, organisation, to become less complex, to pass from a higher to a lower degree of development. As a story, however, a partly supernatural story, it is first-rate in artistic management; those Epicurean niceties only adding to the decorative colour of its central figure, like so many exotic flowers, like the charming scenery and the perpetual, epigrammatic, surprising, yet so natural, conversations, like an atmosphere all about it. All that pleasant accessory detail, taken straight from the culture, the intellectual and social interests, the conventionalities, of the moment, have, in fact, after all, the effect of the better sort of realism, throwing into relief the adroitly-devised supernatural element after the manner of Poe, but with a grace he never reached, which supersedes that earlier didactic purpose, and makes the quite sufficing interest of an excellent story.

We like the hero and, spite of his somewhat unsociable, devotion to his art, Hallward, better than Lord Henry Wotton. He has too much of a not very really refined world in him and about him, and his somewhat cynic opinions, which seem sometimes to be those of the writer, who may, however, have intended Lord Henry as a satiric sketch. Mr. Wilde can hardly have intended him, with his cynic amity of mind and temper, any more than the miserable end of Dorian himself, to figure the motive and tendency of a true Cyrenaic or Epicurean doctrine of life. In contrast with Hallward the artist, whose sensibilities idealise the world around him, the personality of Dorian Gray, above all, into something magnificent and strange, we might say that Lord Henry, and even more the, from the first, suicidal hero, loses too much in life to be a true Epicurean, loses so much in the way of impressions, of pleasant memories, and subsequent hopes, which Hallward, by a really Epicurean economy, manages to secure. It should be said, however, in fairness, that the writer is impersonal; seems not to have identified himself entirely with any one of his characters; and Wotton's cynicism, or whatever it be, at least makes a very clever story possible. He becomes the spoiler of the fair young man, whose bodily form remains un-aged; while his picture, the chef d'oeuvre of the artist Hallward, changes miraculously with the gradual corruption of his soul. How true, what a light on the artistic nature, is the following on actual personalities and their revealing influence in art. We quote it as an example of Mr. Wilde's more serious style.

"I sometimes think that there are only two eras of any importance in the world's history. The first is the appearance of a new medium for art, and the second is the appearance of a new personality for art also. What the invention of oil-painting was to the Venetians, the face of Antinous was to late Greek sculpture, and the face of Dorian Gray will someday be to me. It is not merely that I paint from him, draw from him, sketch from him. Of course I have done all that. But he is much more to me than a model or a sitter. I won't tell you that I am dissatisfied with what I have done of him, or that his beauty is such that Art cannot express it. There is nothing that Art cannot express, and I know that the work I have done, since I met Dorian Gray, is good work, is the best work of my life. But in some curious way ... his personality has suggested to me an entirely new manner in art, an entirely new mode of style. I see things differently. I can now recreate life in a way that was hidden from me before."[33]

Dorian himself, though certainly a quite unsuccessful experiment in Epicureanism, in life as a fine art, is (till his inward spoiling takes visible effect suddenly, and in a moment, at the end of his story) a beautiful creation. But his story is also a vivid, though carefully considered, exposure of the corruption of a soul, with a very plain moral, pushed home, to the effect that vice and crime make people coarse and ugly. General readers, nevertheless, will probably care less for this moral, less for the fine, varied, largely appreciative culture of the writer, in evidence from page to page, than for the story itself, with its adroitly managed supernatural incidents, its almost equally wonderful applications of natural science; impossible, surely, in fact, but plausible enough in fiction. Its interest turns on that very old theme; old because based on some inherent experience or fancy of the human brain, of a double life: of Döppelgänger, not of two persons, in this case, but of the man and his portrait; the latter of which, as we hinted above, changes, decays, is spoiled, while the former, through a long course of corruption, remains, to the outward eye, unchanged, still in all the beauty of a seemingly immaculate youth, "the devil's bargain." But it would be a pity to spoil the reader's enjoyment by further detail. We need only emphasise once more, the skill, the real subtlety of art, the ease and fluidity withal of one telling a story by word of mouth, with which the consciousness of the supernatural is introduced into, and maintained amid, the elaborately conventional, sophisticated, disabused world Mr. Wilde depicts so cleverly, so mercilessly. The special fascination of the piece is, of course, just there, at that point of contrast. Mr. Wilde's work may fairly claim to go with that of Edgar Poe, and with some good French work of the same kind, done, probably, in more or less conscious imitation of it.

THE ATHENAUM IN REVIEWING "The Picture of Dorian Gray,"

in its issue of June 27th, 1891, under the heading of "Novels of the Week," said:

Mr. Oscar Wilde's paradoxes are less wearisome when introduced into the chatter of society than when he rolls them off in the course of his narrative. Some of the conversation in his novel is very smart, and while reading it one has the pleasant feeling, not often to be enjoyed in the company of modern novelists, of being entertained by a person of decided ability. The idea of the book may have been suggested by Balzac's "Peau de Chagrin," and it is none the worse for that. So much may be said for "The Picture of Dorian Gray," but no more, except, perhaps, that the author does not appear to be in earnest. For the rest, the book is unmanly, sickening, vicious (though not exactly what is called "improper"), and tedious.

Mr. R.H. Sherard, in his recently published "Life of Oscar Wilde" (Werner Laurie, 1906), gives some interesting particulars as to the reasons which induced Wilde to write the book, while the views of a French littérateur on "Dorian Gray" may be read in M. André Gide's "Study," a translation of which, by the present editor, was issued from the Holywell Press, Oxford, in 1905.

[32] November 1891.

[33] Pp. 14, 15 (1891 edition).

A critic cannot be fair in the ordinary sense of the word.

THE MORALITY OF "DORIAN GRAY."

The question of the morality of "Dorian Gray" was dealt with very fully
during the trial of the Marquis of Queensberry for libel, and also in the
subsequent trials of Wilde himself, when, the libel action having
collapsed, Wilde was transferred from the witness-box to the dock.

At the trial of Lord Queensberry at the Old Bailey on April 3rd, 1895, Sir
Edward Clarke, in his opening speech for the prosecution, referred to what
he called "an extremely curious count at the end of the plea," namely, that
in July, 1890, Mr. Wilde published, or caused to be published, with his
name upon the title page, a certain immoral and indecent work, with the
title of "The Picture of Dorian Gray," which was intended to be understood
by the readers to describe the relations, intimacies and passions of
certain persons guilty of unnatural practices. That, said Sir Edward, was a
very gross allegation. The volume could be bought at any bookstall in
London. It had Mr. Wilde's name on the title page, and had been published
five years. The story of the book was that of a young man of good birth,
great wealth and great personal beauty, whose friend paints a picture of
him. Dorian Gray expresses the wish that he would remain as in the picture,
while the picture aged with the years. His wish was granted, and he soon
knew that upon the picture and not upon his own face the scars of trouble
and bad conduct were falling. In the end he stabbed the picture and fell
dead. The picture was restored to its pristine beauty, while his friends
find on the floor the body of a hideous old man. "I shall be surprised,"
said Counsel in conclusion, "if my learned friend (Mr. Carson) can pitch
upon any passage in that book which does more than describe as novelists
and dramatists may, nay, must, describe the passions and the fashions of
life."

Lord Queensberry's Counsel was Mr. (now Sir Edward) Carson, M.P. He
proceeded, after Sir Edward's Clarke's speech, to cross-examine Mr. Wilde
on the subject of his writings.

Counsel: You are of opinion, I believe, that there is no such thing as an
immoral book?

Witness: Yes.

Am I right in saying that you do not consider the effect in creating
morality or immorality? Certainly, I do not.

So far as your works are concerned you pose as not being concerned about
morality or immorality? I do not know whether you use the word "pose" in
any particular sense.

It is a favourite word of your own? Is it? I have no pose in this matter.
In writing a play or a book I am concerned entirely with literature, that
is, with art. I aim not at doing good or evil, but in trying to make a
thing that will have some quality of beauty.

After the criticisms that were passed on "Dorian Gray" was it modified a
good deal? No. Additions were made. In one case it was pointed out to me,
not in a newspaper or anything of that sort, but by the only critic of the
century whose opinion I set high, Mr. Walter Pater, that a certain passage
was liable to misconstruction, and I made one addition.

This is in your introduction to "Dorian Gray": "There is no such thing as a moral or an immoral book. Books are well written or badly written. That is all." That expresses my view of art.

Then, I take it that no matter how immoral a book may be, if it is well written it is, in your opinion, a good book? Yes; if it were well written so as to produce a sense of beauty which is the highest sense of which a human being can be capable. If it were badly written it would produce a sense of disgust.

Then a well-written book putting forward perverted moral views may be a good book? No work of art ever puts forward views. Views belong to people who are not artists.

A novel of "a certain kind" might be a good book? I do not know what you mean by "a novel of a certain kind."

Then I will suggest "Dorian Gray" as open to the interpretation of being a novel of that kind. That could only be to brutes and illiterates.

An illiterate person reading "Dorian Gray" might consider it such a novel? The views of illiterates on art are unaccountable. I am concerned only with my view of art. I do not care twopence what other people think of it.

The majority of persons would come under your definition of Philistines and illiterates? I have found wonderful exceptions.

Do you think the majority of people live up to the position you are giving us? I am afraid they are not cultivated enough.

Not cultivated enough to draw the distinction between a good book and a bad book? Certainly not.

The affection and love of the artist of "Dorian Gray" might lead an ordinary individual to believe that it might have a certain tendency? I have no knowledge of the views of ordinary individuals.

You did not prevent the ordinary individual from buying your book? I have never discouraged him.

Mr. Carson then read an extract extending to several pages from "Dorian Gray," using the version as it appeared in Lippincott's Magazine[34], describing the meeting of Dorian Gray and the painter Basil Hallward. "Now, I ask you, Mr. Wilde," added Counsel, "do you consider that that description of the feeling of one man towards another, a youth just grown up, was a proper or an improper feeling?" "I think," replied the author, "it is the most perfect description of what an artist would feel on meeting a beautiful personality which was in some way necessary to his art and life."

Counsel: You think that is a feeling a young man should have towards another?

Witness: Yes, as an artist.

Mr. Carson proceeded to read another long extract. Mr. Wilde asked for a copy, and was given one of the complete edition. Mr. Carson in calling his attention to the place, remarked, "I believe it was left out in the purged edition?"

Witness: I do not call it purged.

Counsel: Yes, I know that; but we will see.

Mr. Carson then read a lengthy passage from "Dorian Gray" as originally published[35], and said, "Do you mean to say that that passage describes the natural feeling of one man towards another?" "It would be the influence produced on an artist by a beautiful personality," was the reply.

Counsel: A beautiful person?

Witness: I said "a beautiful personality." You can describe it as you like. Dorian Gray was a most remarkable personality.

May I take it that you, as an artist, have never known the feeling described here? I have never allowed any personality to dominate my heart.

Then you have never known the feeling you describe? No; it is a work of fiction.

So far as you are concerned you have no experience as to its being a natural feeling? I think it is perfectly natural for any artist to admire intensely and love a young man. It is an incident in the life of almost every artist.

But let us go over it phrase by phrase. "I quite admit that I adored you madly." What do you say to that? Have you ever adored a young man madly? No; not madly. I prefer love; that is a higher form.

Never mind about that. Let us keep down to the level we are at now. I have never given adoration to anybody except myself. (Loud laughter.)

I suppose you think that a very smart thing? Not at all.

Then you never had that feeling? No; the whole idea was borrowed from Shakespeare, I regret to say; yes, from Shakespeare's sonnets.

Mr. Carson, continuing to read: "I adored you extravagantly?" Do you mean financially?

Oh, yes, financially. Do you think we are talking about finance? I do not know what you are talking about.

Don't you? Well, I hope, I shall make myself very plain before I have done. "I was jealous of every one to whom you spoke." Have you ever been jealous of a young man? Never in my life.

"I wanted to have you all to myself." Did you ever have that feeling? No, I should consider it an intense nuisance, an intense bore.

"I grew afraid that the world would know of my idolatry." Why should he grow afraid that the world should know of it? Because there are people in the world who cannot understand the intense devotion, affection and admiration that an artist can feel for a wonderful and beautiful personality. These are the conditions under which we live. I regret them.

These unfortunate people, that have not the high understanding that you have, might put it down to something wrong? Undoubtedly; to any point they chose. I am not concerned with the ignorance of others.

In another passage Dorian Gray receives a book.[36] Was the book to which you refer a moral book? Not well written?

Pressed further upon this point, and as to whether the book he had in mind was not of a certain tendency, Mr. Wilde declined with some warmth to be cross-examined upon the work of another artist. It was, he said, "an impertinence and a vulgarity." He admitted that he had in his mind a French book entitled A Rebours. Mr. Carson wanted to elicit Mr. Wilde's view as to the morality of that book, but Sir Edward Clarke succeeded, on an appeal to the Judge, in stopping any further reference to it.

Counsel then quoted another extract[37] from the Lippincott version of "Dorian Gray," in which the artist tells Dorian of the scandals about him, and finally asks, "Why is your friendship so fateful to young men?" Asked whether the passage in its ordinary meaning did not suggest a certain charge, witness stated that it described Dorian Gray as a man of very corrupt influence, though there was no statement as to the nature of his influence. "But as a matter of fact," he added, "I do not think that one person influences another, nor do I think there is any bad influence in the world."

Counsel: A man never corrupts a youth? I think not.

Nothing could corrupt him? If you are talking of separate ages.

Mr. Carson: No, Sir, I am talking common sense.

Witness: I do not think one person influences another.

You do not think that flattering a young man, making love to him, in fact, would be likely to corrupt him? No.

On the assembling of the court on the following day, Mr. Wilde, who arrived ten minutes late, after saying to the Judge, "My lord, pray accept my apologies for being late in the witness-box," was examined by Sir Edward Clarke. In reference to "Dorian Gray" the witness said: "Mr. Walter Pater wrote me several letters about it, and in consequence of what he said I modified one passage. The book was very widely reviewed, among others by Mr. Pater himself. I wrote a reply to the review that appeared in the Scots Observer."

The subject then dropped.

On the last day of Mr. Wilde's first trial at the Criminal Central Court, May 1st, 1895, the Judge, Mr. Justice Charles, in his summing-up, dealt with "the literary part of the case," and again "Dorian Gray" came under consideration. The Judge said that a very large portion of the evidence of Mr. Wilde at the trial of Lord Queensberry was devoted to what Sir Edward Clarke had called "the literary part of the case." It was attempted to show by cross-examination of Mr. Wilde, as to works he had published, especially in regard to the book called "Dorian Gray," that he was a man of most unprincipled character with regard to the relation of men to boys. His lordship said he had not read that book, and he assumed that the jury had not, but they had been told it was the story of a youth of vicious character, whose face did not reveal the abysses of wretchedness into which he had fallen, but a picture painted by an artist friend revealed all the consequences of his passion. In the end he stabs the picture, whereupon he himself falls dead, and on his vicious face appear all the signs which before had been upon the picture. His lordship did not think that in a criminal case the jury should place any unfavourable inference upon the fact that Mr. Wilde was the author of "Dorian Gray." It was, unfortunately, true that some of their most distinguished and noble-minded writers, who had spent their lives in producing wholesome literature had given to the world books which were painful to persons, of ordinary modesty and decency, to read. Sir Edward Clarke had quoted from Coleridge, "Judge no man by his books," but his lordship would prefer to say "Confound no man with the characters of the persons he creates." Because a novelist put into the mouth of his villain the most abominable sentiments it must not be assumed that he shared them.

It will be remembered that on this occasion the jury were unable to agree on a verdict as to whether Mr. Wilde was guilty or not of the charges brought against him.

In the second trial, which began on May 22nd following, the subject of his books was not mentioned.

[34] Pp. 6-10.

[35] Pp. 57-58.

[36] p. 63, 64.

[37] p. 79.

MR. ROBERT BUCHANAN ON PAGAN VICIOUSNESS.

Mr. Robert Buchanan, the well-known writer, in a letter dated April 23rd, 1895, expressed his own views on this subject in the columns of The Star. Referring to an anonymous correspondent in the same newspaper who had accused Mr. Wilde of "pagan viciousness" this was more than a month before a verdict of "Guilty" had been returned against him, Mr. Buchanan asks, "Has even a writer like this no sense of humour? Does he seriously contend that the paradoxes and absurdities with which Mr. Wilde once amused us were meant as serious attacks on public morality? Two thirds of all Mr. Wilde has written is purely ironical, and it is only because they are now told that the writer is a wicked man that people begin to consider his writings wicked."

"I think," he adds, "I am as well acquainted as most people with Mr. Wilde's works, and I fearlessly assert that they are, for the most part, as innocent as a naked baby. As for the much misunderstood "Dorian Gray," it would be easy to show that it is a work of the highest morality, since its whole purpose is to point out the effect of selfish indulgence and sensuality in destroying the character of a beautiful human soul. But it is useless to discuss these questions with people who are colour-blind. I cordially echo the cry that, failing a little knowledge of literature, a little Christian charity is sorely wanted."

Footnotes. The original footnotes in each case have been retained for authenticity even though in a small number of cases they may no longer be relevant.

Oscar Wilde was an Irish poet, fiction writer and playwright who had a very special life story that made him become considered by many as a sort of martyr of freedom and literature. He had become England's most popular and controversial playwright in the 1880s before he got involved in a court trial in which he was proved guilty of homosexuality, which was a serious crime in Victorian England. After spending two years in prison, an experience that made his psychological and physical health deteriorate, he left the country to seek exile in France and soon died there. Today he is mainly remembered for his fictional masterpiece *The Picture of Dorian Gray* (1890) and also for his dramatic masterpiece *The Importance of Being Earnest* (1895).

Oscar Wilde was born to well-off and intellectual parents in the city of Dublin and received a decent education in which he had always been a distinguished student. His mother Jane Wilde was herself renowned in Ireland as a refined poet. As for Oscar's father, Sir William Wilde, he was a humanitarian medical doctor and a surgeon who left important works of medicine and archeology. Today, he is remembered as one of Ireland's greatest men of science. From an early age, Oscar Wilde became fluent in French and German and then mastered classical schools of philosophy. After an experience at Magdalen College in Oxford, he adopted the philosophical school of aestheticism to become one of its most famous proponents.

After graduation, Wilde's writing activities multiplied. While preaching among literary circles his very famous slogan "Art for art's sake," which objects to all sorts of politicization or moralization of art and literature, he wrote and published collections of poems and short stories. In 1878, Wilde's poem "Ravenna" had made him win the Newdigate Prize. Oscar's first collection of poems was published in 1881 under the title *Poems* and received considerable attention from critics.

He married Constance Llyod in 1884 to have two sons, Cyril and Vyvyan. Constance came from an even wealthier family than his and used to support him, to fund his publications and even to send him money for his personal subsistence at the moments of hardship that characterized his twilight years. Starting from 1882, Wilde lectured in different countries including Ireland, England, Canada and the United States. When he was visiting the latter, his trip was prolonged more than once thanks to the success of his lectures and his published works.

In 1888, Wilde published *The Happy Prince and Other Stories* to be followed by *Lord Arthur Savile's Crime and Other Stories* in 1891. Wilde's short stories were mainly fairy tales for children (originally for his own children), but they can also be enjoyable and instructive for adults. Apart from that, Wilde also started publishing essays and magazine articles for *The Pall Mall Gazette* and *The Woman's World* to serve as the editor of the latter for a number of years.

It was in *Lippincott's Monthly Magazine* that his only novel *The Picture of Dorian Gray* was first published in 1890 to face strong resistance by critics who raised controversies over its homoerotic insinuations. Generally, the story adopts fantastic effects and deals with the theme of the Faustian pact. Dorian is a young man who, after seeing a painting of himself done by a renowned painter, falls in love with it and wishes his youthful beauty depicted in the painting lasts forever. A magical bargain is achieved through which Dorian will physically remain the same while the painting itself will age. Thus, he engages in a life of pleasure and libertinage not caring about age. He is, however, depressed by the mere look at his own aging reflection in the picture as it becomes uglier and uglier. By the end of the novel, he takes a knife and stabs the canvas to kill only himself. Despite the diatribe that some critics launched against the novel's explicit "immorality" and "homosexual allusions," *The Picture of Dorian Gray* has become considered as a refined masterpiece, mainly posthumously in the twentieth century.

The reaction of critics made Wilde even write more essays to explain his artistic vision of aestheticism and to further explain his position according to which art should be considered as only a manifestation of beauty that does not tolerate any moral or political evaluation of the artistic act. In fact, all sorts of moral judgment of art are irrelevant according to Wilde. For him, art is an individualistic act of constant improvisation that should always remain free of all moral and social shackles. The question of whether literature and art in general should take up a moral, social or political role is still debated by today's literary and philosophical circles. During this period, Wilde also wrote other essays on the philosophy of art and politics as well as biographies.

After the publication of the novel, Wilde's plays followed to make him more popular than ever before. His first play was first written in French under the title *Salomé* (1891). It was followed by *Lady Windermere's Fan* in 1892, *A Woman of No Importance* in 1893, *An Ideal Husband* in 1895 and *The Importance of Being Earnest* in the same year. Most of these plays were social comedies or comedies of manners that painted the Victorian society, parodied and satirized its manners, etiquette and social hypocrisy. Wilde's plays, which remained on stages for long and enabled the author to make considerable fortunes, served as a mirror that made the Victorian audience laugh at the contradictions and paradoxes in which they found themselves. The dialogues were stuffed with witty remarks, humorous misunderstandings and sharp quips that could only inspire appreciation among the people that they criticized. Wilde had still to face the dissatisfaction of Victorian diehard conservatives, though.

By that time, Wilde was constantly moving between Paris and London where he attended his premières and frequented literary salons. Unfortunately, the 1890s did not only bring fame and financial prosperity to Oscar Wilde, but also much trouble that would ultimately ruin him. All started when he made acquaintance with young Alfred Douglas in 1891. They engaged in an adventurous homosexual relationship, a relationship that was suspected by Alfred's atheist yet conservative father, the Marquis of Queensberry.

Wilde's relationship with Douglas was romantic and biographers note that the prosperous rising star used to pamper his partner, realizing all his dreams. Though much younger than the celebrated playwright, it was Douglas who introduced Wilde to the world of male debauchery and prostitution. Meanwhile, Douglas's father was haunting the couple, trying to find out about their secret. When he finally became sure of the affair, he explicitly threatened Wilde.

The Marquis of Queensberry had never thought of suing Wilde, however, was it not for the fact that Wilde himself started by prosecuting him. The story began when Queensberry defamed Wilde among his circles by describing him as a homosexual and a sodomite. Wilde's mistake was to prosecute Queensberry for libel while he knew that it was very easy to find proofs of his homosexual behavior and that this was criminalized by British law. During trial, Queensberry's lawyers were trying to prove that their client's claims were founded in order to absolve him from the accusation of libel. They finally succeeded in their mission. Right after the end of the trial, a warrant was issued for Wilde's arrest, his crime being "gross indecency".

Having lost a lot of money on the trial and lawyers, Wilde had also to pay all Queensberry's expenses before he was sentenced to a two-year imprisonment with hard labor. The experience of prison gravely affected him both psychologically and physically. Despite the time and idleness that prison usually offers, his literary activity decreased greatly. In fact, he only succeeded in finishing one work while in prison. This work was intended to be a letter to Douglas that Wilde entitled *De Profundis* (Latin for "from the depths"). The long letter, which was later published in book form to become among Wilde's most read works, spoke about the author's experience during the trials. The letter also displayed a feeling of remorse. Wilde claimed that his mistake was that he had wished to experience all sorts of earthly pleasure when pleasure had wrongly been the sole purpose of his life.

Wilde even developed religious sentiments in prison and wished to have a retreat at the Catholic Church after being released, yet this was not accepted. When he left the prison in 1897, he immediately decided to leave the country for France where he lived almost alone after having lost his money and the luster of fame. He was only frequented by a small number of intimate friends and received money for subsistence from his wife, though they were officially separated. In Paris, Wilde wrote his last work before he passed away. This was a long poem entitled *The Ballad of Reading Gaol*. The verse recounts the horrors of prison.

On November 30th, 1900, Oscar Wilde died of cerebral meningitis in the French capital. He rests today at the Père Lachaise Cemetery where he is visited by thousands of his readers and fans every year. Today, as misconceptions about Wilde's life and personal choices have changed, his works as well as his career have helped raise him to the status of legends.

www.ingramcontent.com/pod-product-compliance
Lightning Source LLC
Chambersburg PA
CBHW060059050426
42448CB00011B/2531